Contents

GW00418707

Introduction

The Abacus model

The Abacus materials are designed and written to allow for a daily, structured mathematics lesson:

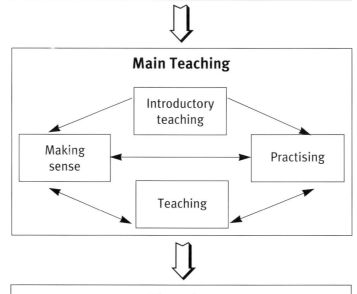

Each day's teaching begins with a whole class mental maths activity. These are presented in the **Mental Warm-up Activities** book.

The main part of the lesson is supported by the **Teacher Cards**:

- the front of each card gives support for whole class teaching for the first day of a topic
- the back of each card gives advice on further teaching for subsequent days and references to the practical activities included in this book. References to relevant **Textbook** pages and **Photocopy Masters** are also provided.

Each lesson is rounded-off with a plenary session. Guidance on key points to reiterate, common misconceptions to look out for, and whole class activities are included on the back of each Teacher Card.

Activity Book

The activities in this book are intended as follow-up to the introductory teaching. Each unit of the programme is supported by a range of activities covering different styles, numbers of children, resources etc.

Each activity includes the following information:

- Appropriate number of children, e.g. pairs, 3-4 children, whole class.

- A list of relevant materials. Any 'specialist' resources, e.g. number grids, number tracks … are provided as Photocopy Masters at the back of the book. Number lines, number cards, place-value cards etc are also available separately in the **Resource Bank**.

- Level of difficulty, indicated by the following codes:

    - basic work

    - for all children

    - enrichment and extension.

- Learning points are also provided, drawing on the teaching objectives from the Teacher Card. These learning points will assist the teacher in directing the group and making informal assessments. They are also useful as key points to highlight in the plenary session – it may be beneficial to give the children some points to consider when setting up the activity. This will give them a clear focus for the outcome of the activity and any key points they might raise in the plenary session.

- A number of ICT activities are included (these assume some prior knowledge of relevant software, e.g. spreadsheets).

Whole class work

Following the initial teaching input, it is often a useful strategy to carry out some immediate consolidation, with the whole class or large group, working on an appropriate activity. Many of the units include a whole class activity specifically written to support this strategy. Such activities are indicated by the icon:

We suggest that following the initial teaching input for the whole class activity, the children are arranged in pairs or small groups, and work independently for a short period exploring or consolidating their learning. These activities will sometimes lead into the plenary session, where the topic can be rounded-off with a discussion about what the children have learned and any difficulties they encountered.

Classroom management

When working with groups it is important to have a manageable number of groups (about four is ideal). It may be appropriate for one or two of those groups to be working from a Textbook or Photocopy Master page. You may decide to have more than one group working on the same activity concurrently. You should try to focus your attention on one or two groups, working intensively with them, directing, discussing, evaluating etc. The Abacus model assists management by ensuring that all the children are broadly working within the same topic, at the same time as providing differentiated work through the activities in this book and the Photocopy Masters.

The activities are written with enough detail covering resources and learning outcomes (as well as the description of the activities themselves) to allow any support staff to manage easily groups you are not working with directly.

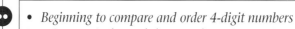

ACTIVITY 1
Whole class, in pairs

- *Beginning to compare and order 4-digit numbers*
Number cards (0 to 9) (PCM 10), a place-value board (thousands, hundreds, tens, units) (PCM 23)
Select four number cards at random, e.g. 4, 3, 6 and 9. Ask the children to select the same four cards. The children make different 4-digit numbers according to your instructions, e.g. *Make the largest number* (9643); *make the smallest number* (3469); *make the smallest even number* (3496); *make a number with 6 in the hundreds column* (e.g. 4639); *make a number more than 6500* (e.g. 6943), and so on. Discuss the correct number each time. Choose four different cards and repeat.

ACTIVITY 2
3-4 children

- *Reading and writing a 4-digit number*
Place-value cards (thousands, hundreds, tens, units) (PCMs 1 to 5)
Shuffle the cards separately and place them face down in four piles. One child picks and hides one card from each pile to make a 4-digit number. The child says the number, e.g. *Four thousand, five hundred and seventy-one* and the other children write it down. The first child shows their cards so that the others can check their number. Repeat several times with other children choosing cards.

ACTIVITY 3
2 pairs

- *Partitioning a 4-digit number into thousands, hundreds, tens and units*
Place-value cards (thousands, hundreds, tens, units) (PCMs 1 to 5)
Shuffle the cards separately and place them face down in four piles. One pair takes one card from each pile, and secretly makes a 4-digit number. They read the number, e.g. *Four thousand, six hundred and ninety-one*. The other pair writes it down in thousands, hundreds, tens and units, i.e. '4000 + 600 + 90 + 1'. The first pair then reveals the cards to check. Repeat several times, swapping roles.

ACTIVITY 4
3-4 children

- *Recognising the value of each digit in a 4-digit number*
Two sets of number cards (0 to 9) (PCM 10), counters
Shuffle the cards and deal four to each child. Each child secretly arranges their cards to make a 4-digit number. Ask them to reveal their numbers. The child with the largest thousands digit collects four counters, the child with the largest hundreds digit collects three counters, the child with the largest tens digit collects two counters, and the child with the largest units digit collects one counter. In the event of a tie, no counters are collected. Repeat for ten rounds.

ACTIVITY 5
3-4 children

- *Writing a 4-digit number in words*
Two sets of number cards (0 to 9) (PCM 10)
Shuffle the cards and deal four to each child. Ask them to create a 4-digit number, e.g. 4716. Each child then writes the number in words, i.e. 'four thousand, seven hundred and sixteen'. They check each other's spelling and count the number of letters needed to write the number, i.e. 34. The children then collect the cards and deal them out again and repeat.

ACTIVITY 6
3-4 children

- *Creating a 4-digit number from thousands, hundreds, tens and units*
Game 1: 'Cube Collector', Base Ten material, a dice, counters
(See instructions on the card.)

Addition/subtraction

ACTIVITY 1
Whole class, in pairs

- *Adding a 1-digit number to a 2-digit number to make the next ten*

Large number grid (1 to 100), number cards (10 to 99, excluding multiples of 10) (PCMs 10 to 16)

Shuffle the cards and place them in a pile face down. Each pair draws four circles and writes a 2-digit multiple of ten in each one. Turn over a card and read out the number. *What is the next ten?* If any pair has that multiple of ten written in a circle, they must tell you how many must be added to the card number to make that ten. If they are correct, they can cross out that multiple. Turn over another card and repeat. The first pair to cross out all their numbers wins.

ACTIVITY 2
3 children

- *Adding a 1-digit number to a 2-digit number to make the next ten*

Number grid (1 to 100) (PCM 19)

One child secretly writes a 2-digit number on a small piece of paper, folds the paper and writes on the top the number which adds to their number to make the next ten. E.g. they write '43' on the paper, fold it and then write '7' on the top. The other children take turns to guess the number which is hidden. The child who guesses correctly has to say the next ten, e.g. *Fifty*. If they are correct, it is their turn to write secretly the next number. Repeat several times.

ACTIVITY 3
3 children

- *Adding a 1-digit number to a 2-digit number to make the next ten*

Number cards (10 to 99, excluding the multiples of 10) (PCMs 10 to 16), two sets of number cards (1 to 9), (PCM 10)

Spread out the 10 to 99 number cards face down. Shuffle both sets of 1 to 9 number cards together and place them in a pile face down. One child turns over the top card in the pile. The children take turns to turn over one of the cards which are spread out. The child who first turns over a card which will add to the single-digit number card to make a multiple of ten must say the next ten. If they are correct, they keep the card they turned over. E.g. the card on the top of the pile is number 9. One child eventually turns over 31 and says *Forty*. They then keep the 31 number card. Turn all the 2-digit number cards back face down and place the single-digit number card at the bottom of the pile. Repeat with another child turning over the top card. Continue until one child has eight cards.

ACTIVITY 4
Pairs

- *Adding a 1-digit number to a 2-digit number to make the next ten*

A dice

One child rolls the dice and writes down the numbers rolled. They continue rolling until they throw a six, when they must stop and say *Halt!* While that child is rolling the dice, their partner writes as many additions to 10 as they can. They score ten for each correctly-written addition. When a six has been thrown, the children check the scores then swap roles and play again. Continue until each child has had at least three turns writing the additions.

ACTIVITY 5
3 children

- *Adding two, three, four or five coins*
- *Knowing what to add to a 2-digit amount less than 50p to make 50p*

Five coins (1p, 2p, 5p, 10p, 20p)

Spread out the coins in a line. One child takes one, two, three, four or five coins. They add the coins and write the amount. They must then work out how much more they need to make 50p and write it down. The coins are then replaced and another child takes some coins. However, they cannot take the same amount as the previous child. They too write down the amount they have, and work out how much more will make 50p. The children continue, taking a different amount each time. How many different amounts can they take?

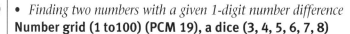

ACTIVITY 1
Whole class, in pairs

- *Finding two numbers with a given 1-digit number difference*
Number grid (1 to100) (PCM 19), a dice (3, 4, 5, 6, 7, 8)
Roll the dice and announce the number thrown. The children work in pairs to find two numbers on their grid which have a difference of that number. However, the two numbers must not have the same tens digit. E.g. If the dice throw is 4, the children could choose 17 and 21 but not 21 and 25. Each pair writes the matching subtraction, e.g. '21 – 17 = 4'. Repeat the activity several times but point out that the children cannot write a pair of numbers they have written before.

ACTIVITY 2
Pairs

- *Finding the difference between two 2-digit numbers which are close together*
Place-value cards (10 to 90) (PCM 1), two sets of number cards (1 to 9) (PCM 10), a dice
Spread out the tens and units cards, face up. One child chooses a tens card. The other child must take a card which is ten more or less than that card. The children then each throw the dice and take a units card to match their number thrown. They work together to calculate the difference between each pair of numbers. They write the matching subtraction. They repeat the activity, with the other child taking the first tens card. Continue, playing several times.

ACTIVITY 3
2-3 children

- *Recognising pairs of numbers with a difference of 10 or 9*
Number cards (1 to 30) (PCMs 10 to 12)
Spread out the cards face up. The children take turns to select a pair of cards with a difference of ten. E.g. they could select 3 and 13. If the difference is indeed ten, they keep their cards. How many pairs can they each collect? Repeat the activity, this time asking the children to look for cards with a difference of nine.

ACTIVITY 4
3 children

- *Recognising patterns in differences between 2-digit numbers*
On a sheet of paper, the first child writes '30', the second child writes the number five more to the right of the 30 and the third child writes the number five less to the left of the 30. The third child then writes '31' below the 30. The first child writes the number five more to the right, and the second child writes the number five less to the left and then writes '32' below 31. The children continue, creating a table of numbers, finishing when one of them writes '40'. Can they see a pattern in the units digits of the numbers? They then repeat the activity, starting with 30 again, but this time writing the number six more to the right and the number six less to the left. They continue again until they reach 40. They repeat for numbers which are seven more and less, and so on. What units patterns do they spot?

N4 Addition/subtraction

ACTIVITY 1
Whole class, in five teams

- *Recalling addition pairs of multiples of 5 to 100*

Fives cards (5 to 100) (PCMs 10 to 16)

Shuffle the cards and place them in a pile face down. Give each team a range of numbers, e.g. team A has 1-20, team B has 21-40, etc. Choose a child to turn over a card. *What goes with that number to make 100?* The team whose range includes that number must stand up. Pick a child in that team. Show them the card and ask them what number goes with the card number to make 100. The child has to say the correct answer, and say why. E.g. the card is 35. The child says, *Sixty-five, because thirty-five and five more is forty, and sixty makes one hundred.* A correct answer scores five points. (A less good explanation or a hesitant answer might score three points.) Continue until one team has 20 points.

ACTIVITY 2
3 children

- *Recalling addition pairs to 100*

Coins (nine 10ps, ten 1ps), a feely bag

One child removes a number of 10p and 1p coins from the bag. The others count out how much they have. They write down the amount, e.g. '36p'. The other two children work together to decide what number will add to that amount to make £1, e.g. 64p. They write down the amount and then check their answer by counting the money left in the bag. Were they correct? They repeat the activity several times, taking turns to remove the money from the bag.

ACTIVITY 3
3 children

- *Recalling addition pairs of multiples of 100 to 1000*

Number cards (1 to 9) (PCM 10)

Shuffle the cards and place them in a pile face down. One child takes a card and keeps the number a secret. They secretly write down that number of hundreds and work out what number of hundreds must be added to make 1000. They write the addition, and then say the matching number to the other children. E.g. if the child takes 4, they write down '400 + 600 = 1000' and say *Six hundred.* The others then discuss and agree the number they think is on the card. The first child then reveals the card number. Repeat the activity with the children changing roles. Continue until all the cards have been taken.

ACTIVITY 4
3 children

- *Recalling addition pairs of multiples of 10 to 100*

Two sets of tens cards (10 to 90) (PCMs 10 to 16)

Spread out the cards face down. Each child takes a card without showing the others. One child looks at their card and asks the other two if they have the corresponding card to total 100. E.g. if they have 40, they ask the other two if they have 60. If the answer is yes, they take the 60 and keep the pair of cards. If the answer is no, the second child asks the others if they have a corresponding card to make 100. Any unpaired cards are returned. Repeat the activity with a different child starting the process. Continue until all the cards are paired.

ACTIVITY 5
Pairs

- *Recalling addition pairs to 100*

Place-value cards (tens and units) (PCMs 1 to 3), extra number card (5)

The children use the cards to lay out as many pairs of numbers as possible which total 100. E.g. they could lay out 64 + 36. *Can you use all the cards? Are there several ways of doing this?*

ACTIVITY 6
3 children

- *Recalling addition pairs to 100*

Game 2: 'Balloon Race', counters, a coin, cubes

(See instructions on the card.)

ACTIVITY 1
Whole class, in pairs

• *Adding several 1-digit numbers*
Two sets of large number cards (1 to 9), Blu-tack
Shuffle the two sets of cards together and place them in a pile face down. Each pair of children divides their page into a left- and a right-hand side. They write three numbers between 20 and 30 on the right-hand side of their paper. Take five cards from the pile and stick them on the board. Each pair adds the card numbers and agrees a total. They write the total on the left-hand side of their page. If the total matches one of the numbers on the right-hand side they score ten points. Return the five cards to the bottom of the pile and repeat several times.

ACTIVITY 2
3 children

• *Adding several 1-digit numbers*
Four sets of number cards (2 to 9) (PCM 10), interlocking cubes, a timer
Set the timer to 20 seconds. One child turns over four cards. The others start the timer and the first child has to add the four cards as fast as they can. If they manage to do this before the timer runs out, they take five cubes. Repeat with a different child turning over the cards. Make the activity easier or harder by asking the children to turn over three or five cards, or changing the time allowed.

ACTIVITY 3
3 children

• *Recognising number pairs to 10 and adding several numbers*
Two sets of number cards (1 to 10) (PCM 10), interlocking cubes, a timer
Shuffle the cards and spread them out face down. Set the timer to 30 seconds. One child starts the timer while another turns over a card and writes the bond to ten. They do this as many times as they can before the timer finishes. The other two children check that they have written the correct number for each card. For the bonds that are correct, the child can add together the card numbers to give them their total score. E.g. the child turns over a 4 and writes '6', turns over a 7 and writes '3', turns over an 8 and writes '2' and turns over a 6 and writes '3'. They are correct on the first three cards, and wrong on the last. They therefore score 4 + 7 + 8 which is 19. Repeat the activity several times with the children changing roles.

ACTIVITY 4
3 children

• *Adding several 1-digit numbers of 6 or under*
• *Recognising tens*
3 dice, counters, interlocking cubes
One child rolls the three dice together. They add together the three numbers. If two of the numbers add to make ten, they can take five counters. If all three dice add to make ten, they can take ten counters. The others check that the child has added the dice correctly. If correct, the child can take three cubes. Repeat the activity several times with the children changing roles.

ACTIVITY 5
3 children

• *Adding several consecutive 1-digit and 2-digit numbers*
The first child writes '1 + 2 = 3', the second child writes '2 + 3 + 4 = 9', and the third child writes '3 + 4 + 5 + 6 = 18'. The children continue for several more rounds. They then explore the patterns made by adding these consecutive numbers.

N6 Properties of number

ACTIVITY 1
Whole class, in pairs

• *Counting in twenty-fives*
Large number cards (25, 50, 75, 100, 125, 150, 175, 200, 225, 250)
Each pair writes down three numbers between 1 and 10. Turn over a card and show it to the children, e.g. 175. *How many twenty-fives do I count to reach this number?* Count in unison, raising one finger for each number: *Twenty-five, fifty, seventy-five, one hundred ......* etc. *We counted seven twenty-fives.* Any pair who had written down 7 can cross it out. Continue playing until several pairs have crossed out all their numbers.

ACTIVITY 2
3 children

• *Counting in fifties*
Two dice
One child rolls the two dice together without letting the other children see what they have rolled. They add the two numbers and count silently in fifties that many times. E.g. they throw a 3 and a 4, add these to make 7, and count 50, 100, 150, 200, 250, 300, 350. They tell the other children the last number in the count. The others have to work out and declare the total of the two dice numbers. E.g. They count in fifties to 350 and say *Seven.* Repeat the activity several times with the other children taking turns to roll the dice.

ACTIVITY 3
3 children

• *Counting in tens, hundreds, fifties and twenty-fives*
Two sets of number cards (2 to 10) (PCM 10)
Shuffle the cards and spread them out face down. One child turns over a card and counts from zero in as many steps as the card number, in either hundreds, fifties, twenty-fives or tens. E.g. the child takes the 4 card and counts four steps in hundreds, *One hundred, two hundred, three hundred, four hundred.* The other children have to say what size steps the child was counting in, i.e. *hundreds.* Repeat several times with the children swapping roles.

ACTIVITY 4
3 children

• *Counting in tens, hundreds, fifties and twenty-fives*
One child writes a 3-digit number. The other children have to work out the lowest 1- or 2-digit number they would have started with had they counted in twenty-fives and reached that 3-digit number. E.g. the child writes '365', and the other two count back in twenty-fives to arrive at 15. Repeat several times with the children taking turns to write the 3-digit number. Repeat for counting back in tens, hundreds and fifties.

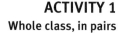

ACTIVITY 1
Whole class, in pairs

• *Recognising the concept of multiplication as an array*
Squared paper, scissors
Each pair draws a rectangle with sides up to eight units in length and cuts it out. Choose one of the rectangles, show the class, and say its measurements, e.g. *Five rows of three squares*. The other children draw and cut out this rectangle, and write a matching multiplication on it, i.e. '5 × 3 = 15'. Repeat, choosing different pairs of children.

ACTIVITY 2
3 children

• *Multiplying using rows of cubes of equal size*
Interlocking cubes, a calculator
One child builds some towers of interlocking cubes which are equal in length. They then lay the towers together in rows. The other two children look at them and decide how many rows there are, and how many cubes in each row. They then write this as a multiplication, e.g. '5 × 3 =' . The first child enters the multiplication on the calculator and then counts the cubes to see if the number matches the answer on the calculator. If it matches, the children write the answer, i.e. '5 × 3 = 15'. The children repeat the activity ten times, sharing the roles.

ACTIVITY 3
3-4 children

• *Finding different multiplications (pairs of factors) for a given product*
Number cards (1 to 30) (PCMs 10 to 12), interlocking cubes, squared paper
Shuffle the cards and place them face down in a pile. One child turns over the top card. All the children write down as many multiplications as they can which have that answer, e.g. '28 is 4 × 7, 7 × 4, 28 × 1, 1 × 28, 2 × 14 and 14 × 2'. The children check each other's answers and take one cube each for every correct multiplication. They can check, if necessary, by drawing rectangles on squared paper. The children repeat the activity until all the cards have gone, taking turns to reveal the top card. *Who has the most cubes?*

ACTIVITY 4
3-4 children

• *Recognising multiplication as repeated addition*
Number cards (2 to 6) (PCM 10), number cards (10 to 30) (PCMs 10 to 12), a calculator, counters
Shuffle the cards separately and place them face down in two piles. One child turns over the top card from each pile, e.g. 5 and 21. Using these numbers, all the children write down a multiplication and the answer, using repeated addition to help them, e.g. '5 × 21 = 21 + 21 + 21 + 21 + 21 = 105'. The children check each other's answers, then use a calculator to check that they are correct. All those with a correct answer collect a counter. Replace the cards and repeat with another pair of cards. The winner is the first to collect eight counters.

ACTIVITY 5
2 children

• *Recognising the concept of multiplication as an array*
• *Finding all the pairs of factors of a given number*
Squared paper
The children work together to draw as many different rectangles with an area of 36 squares as they can. They write down all the multiplications, e.g. '6 × 6 = 36, 3 × 12 = 36, ...'. Repeat the activity, this time drawing rectangles with 60 squares.

N8 Multiplication/division

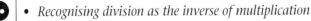

ACTIVITY 1
Whole class, in pairs

• *Recognising division as the inverse of multiplication*
Write a division on the board, e.g. '28 ÷ 4 ='. The children write down the division with the answer alongside. To find the answer, they count quietly in fours to see how many fours make 28. Check the answer together, by counting in fours as a whole class. Those pairs with a correct answer score one point. Repeat for different divisions until one pair has ten points.

ACTIVITY 2
3 children

• *Recognising division as the inverse of multiplication*
• *Dividing by grouping*
Number cards (multiples of 3, 4 and 6) (PCMs 10 to 14), interlocking cubes, tables lists (PCM 24)
Shuffle the cards and place them face down in a pile. One child chooses a card, e.g. 27, says which table it is in, i.e. ×3 table, and builds cubes in rows to match the multiple, i.e. nine rows of three. The child writes the matching division, i.e. '27 ÷ 3 = 9'. If the answer is correct, the child keeps the card. The children continue, taking turns, until all the cards have gone.

ACTIVITY 3
3-4 children

• *Recalling division facts*
• *Dividing by grouping*
Division cards (PCMs 39 to 42), interlocking cubes, tables lists (PCM 24)
Shuffle the cards and place them face down in a pile. The children take turns to turn over the top card, e.g. 21 ÷ 3 and use the cubes to make groups of three. The other two try to divide mentally, recalling the ×3 facts or the ×3 table. Each child secretly writes down their answer. They then show each other their answers, check the number of cubes, and finally check with the tables lists. Replace the card at the bottom of the pile and repeat until all the cards have been used.

ACTIVITY 4
3-4 children

• *Recognising numbers which divide into a given number*
• *Recalling division facts*
Tables lists (PCM 24), number cards (1 to 60) (PCMs 10 to 14), interlocking cubes
Shuffle the cards and place them face down in a pile. The children take turns to turn over a card, e.g. 27, then say a number from 2 to 19 which divides into it, e.g. *Nine*. They check the tables lists to see if they are correct, and if so, take a matching number of cubes. They continue until one child has collected 30 cubes.

ACTIVITY 5
3 children

• *Recalling division facts*
• *Recognising the concept of a prime number*
Number cards (1 to 40) (PCMs 10 to 13)
Place the cards face up in rows of ten from 1 to 40. The children work together to find the prime numbers from 1 to 40, i.e. the numbers which can only be divided exactly by themselves and 1, e.g. 11. *How many of the prime numbers are even?*

ACTIVITY 6
3-4 children

• *Recalling division facts*
Game 3: 'Star Turn', a dice, counters, interlocking cubes
(See instructions on the card.)

 N9 Multiplication/division

ACTIVITY 1
Whole class, in pairs

- *Recalling multiplication facts*

Choose a multiple, e.g. 4. Write a set of ×4 multiplication facts on the board, e.g. '7 × 4, 3 × 4, 8 × 4, ...', as many as there are pairs of children. Each pair chooses one of them and writes the multiplication, together with their answer. Go through each fact in turn, checking which pairs have chosen it, and agreeing the answer. Count together in fours, checking how many counts of four are needed for each fact. Repeat the activity, with each pair choosing a different ×4 fact. Do the activity again with a different multiple, e.g. ×5.

ACTIVITY 2
3 children

- *Recognising multiples on a number line*
- *Recalling the multiples of a number*

10-division number lines (PCM 20)

The children choose a multiple, e.g. 3, and write '0' and '30' below the ends of the number line. They then write numbers for each division, also below the line. They cover up all the numbers below the line, and try to say the position of each division. Repeat for different multiples on new number lines.

ACTIVITY 3
3-4 children

- *Recalling division facts*
- *Recognising division facts*

Division cards (÷3, ÷4) (PCMs 39, 40), tables lists (PCM 24)

Shuffle the cards and spread them out face down on the table. The children take turns to reveal a card, and try to give the answer to the multiplication. They then use the tables list to check their answer. If they are correct, they keep the card. If not, they replace it face down in a position not seen by the others. When all the cards have been collected, see who has the most. Reshuffle the cards and repeat.

ACTIVITY 4
3 children

- *Recalling multiplication facts*

Multiplication cards (×3, ×4) (PCMs 35, 36), tables lists (PCM 24)

Shuffle the cards and place them face down in a pile. One child turns over a card and shows it to the other children who have one guess only at the answer. The first to give the answer correctly keeps the card. The children can use the tables lists as a check. Repeat with the children swapping roles until all the cards have been taken. Who has collected the most?

ACTIVITY 5
2-3 children

- *Recognising multiples of a number*
- *Recognising and recalling multiples of 10*

10-division number lines (PCM 20)

The children write the first ten multiples of a chosen number, e.g. 4, above one of the number lines. They then use these to write the multiples of 40 below the line. Can they say the multiples of 40 in order? Can they say them randomly? Repeat for a different multiple on another number line.

ACTIVITY 6
Pairs

- *Recalling multiplication facts*

Spreadsheet software, multiplication cards (×2, ×3, ×4, ×5) (PCMs 35 to 38), counters

Prepare a spreadsheet file using the formula '=A1*B1 ...' in Column C. Shuffle the multiplication cards and put them face down in a pile. The children take turns to pick a card and give the answer. The children enter the numbers on their card in Columns A and B, check the answer (which will appear in Column C) and collect a counter if correct. The first child to collect five counters is the winner.

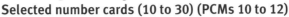 **Multiplication/division**

ACTIVITY 1
Whole class, in pairs

- *Doubling numbers up to 30*
Selected number cards (10 to 30) (PCMs 10 to 12)
Shuffle the cards and show one of them to the class, e.g. 24. One child in each pair is responsible for doubling the tens, and the other for doubling the units. Each pair then combines their two numbers to obtain their double. Discuss the answers. Each pair collects one point for a correct answer. Repeat for different numbers, allowing the children to alternate for doubling the tens and units.

ACTIVITY 2
3-4 children

- *Doubling numbers up to 10*
Number cards (1 to 10) (PCM 10), interlocking cubes
Shuffle the cards and spread them out face down. One child takes a card and builds a tower with that many cubes. A second child builds a tower with the same number of cubes. The third child writes the card number and doubles it. The children count the number of cubes in both towers. Is the third child correct? The children continue, sharing the roles, until all the cards have been used. The children may then be able to progress to numbers beyond 10.

ACTIVITY 3
3-4 children

- *Doubling 2-digit numbers with a units digit 5 or less*
Number cards (1 to 15, 20 to 25, 30 to 35) (PCMs 10 to 12), Base Ten equipment
Shuffle the cards and place them face down in a pile. The children take turns to take a card and attempt to say its double. They then take double the card number of Base Ten, checking each other's Base Ten to see if they are correct. If the answer is correct, the child keeps the card; if not, the card is replaced at the bottom of the pile. Continue until all the cards have been used. Who has collected the most cards?

ACTIVITY 4
3-4 children

- *Halving even numbers up to 100*
Number cards (even numbers 20 to 100) (PCMs 10 to 16), coins (10p, 1p), counters
Shuffle the cards and place them face down in a pile. One child turns over a card, e.g. 56 and all the children attempt to write its half. Together they collect a matching number of pence, i.e. 56p and then split it into two equal amounts, changing a 10p coin for ten 1p coins, if necessary. They count the amount in each half and then check that this matches the answers. The children collect a counter if their answer is correct. Continue, replacing the money and choosing different cards. Who collects the most counters?

ACTIVITY 5
2-4 children

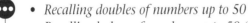

- *Recalling doubles of numbers up to 50*
- *Recalling halves of numbers up to 50 (including odd numbers)*
Number cards (1 to 50) (PCMs 10 to 13)
Shuffle the cards and deal one to each child. Without showing the other children their card, they write its double and its half. If the number is odd, e.g. 31, they record the half as '15$\frac{1}{2}$'. Each card is then passed to the right, and the children write the doubles and halves of the new numbers. Continue until all the children have received each card. The children then check each other's answers. Repeat with a different set of cards. The activity can be extended to larger numbers if required.

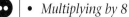

ACTIVITY 1
Whole class, in pairs

- *Multiplying by 8*
Number cards (1 to 10) (PCM 10), ×8 table list (PCM 24)
Shuffle the cards and place them face down in a pile. The children take turns to reveal a card, e.g. 3, and say the number of eights, i.e. *Three eights are twenty-four.* They check by recalling three fours, then doubling the result. They also check by chanting the multiples of 8 and by using the ×8 table.

ACTIVITY 2
2-3 children

- *Creating the ×8 multiplication table*
2 cm-squared paper
The children write '1, 2, 3, 4, 5, 6, 7, 8' along the first row of the paper, then '9, 10, 11, 12, 13, 14, 15, 16' along the second row, and so on. They then write the multiplication table, writing '1 × 8 = 8' beside the first row, '2 × 8 = 16' beside the second row, and so on to complete the table.

ACTIVITY 3
3-4 children

- *Multiplying by 8*
Blank 5 × 5 grid (PCM 26) filled in with 1-digit numbers at random, blank 5 × 5 grid (PCM 26), a calculator
The children work together to multiply each grid number by 8, and record the answers in the matching spaces on the blank grid. They can recall their ×4 facts, then double these if necessary. They can use a calculator to check their answers.

ACTIVITY 4
3-4 children

- *Recalling the ×8 facts*
Multiplication cards ×8 (PCMs 37, 38), interlocking cubes (in towers of 8), counters
Shuffle the cards and place them face down in a pile. The children take turns to turn over a card, say and then write the complete multiplication. They can use the cubes to check their answer. If they are correct, they take a counter. They check each other's answers. When all the cards have been used, repeat.

ACTIVITY 5
2-3 children

- *Linking ×8 facts to ÷8 facts*
Multiplication and division cards (×8, ÷8) (PCMs 37, 38, 41, 42), ×8 table list (PCM 24)
Shuffle the multiplication cards and place them in a pile face down. Spread out the division cards face up. The children take turns to turn over a multiplication card and say the answer. They then look for the matching division card. They can use the table list to check. If correct, they take both cards. Finally, they place all the cards in ascending order, matching multiplications and divisions. Repeat.

ACTIVITY 6
3-4 children

- *Linking ÷8 facts to multiples of 8*
Number grid (1 to 100) (PCM 19), a dice, counters (in 3/4 colours)
The children each place a counter on 1 on the grid. They take turns to throw the dice and move a matching number of spaces. If they land on a multiple of 8, they leave the counter there, and say the matching division, e.g. *Forty-eight divided by eight is six.* On their next turn they use a new counter. When they all reach 100, the winner is the child with the most counters on the grid.

ACTIVITY 7
3-4 children

- *Multiplying by 8 by doubling, then doubling again, then doubling again*
Number cards (10 to 30) (PCM 10 to 12), a calculator, counters
Shuffle the cards and place them in a pile face down. One child turns over a card and they all multiply the number by 8 by doubling the number, doubling again, then doubling again. They write down their answer, and check it with the calculator. Those with a correct answer collect a counter. Repeat several times until one child has ten counters.

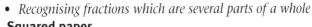 N12 Fractions/decimals

ACTIVITY 1
Whole class, in pairs

• *Recognising fractions which are several parts of a whole*
Squared paper
The children draw eight 2 × 4 grids on the squared paper, and colour and label each one to show the eighths – $\frac{1}{8}$, $\frac{2}{8}$, $\frac{3}{8}$, ... $\frac{7}{8}$. They then choose an appropriate-sized grid to show either sixths (six 2 × 3 grids) or tenths (ten 2 × 5 grids) and colour and label those.

ACTIVITY 2
2-3 children

• *Recognising the fractions $\frac{1}{2}$, $\frac{1}{4}$ and $\frac{3}{4}$ by shading a grid*
Fraction cards ($\frac{1}{2}$, $\frac{1}{4}$, $\frac{3}{4}$) (PCM 31), six 2 × 4 grids, felt-tip pens (in 2/3 colours), interlocking cubes
Shuffle the cards and place them face down in a pile. The children take turns to turn over a card, choose a grid, and colour a matching fraction. The card is put back in the pile and the cards are shuffled. The children continue taking a card and colouring in a fraction of a grid. If a child completes a grid, they take a cube (the exact fraction must be used to complete a grid). When all the grids have been coloured, repeat with another set of grids. Who has the most cubes?

ACTIVITY 3
2-4 children

• *Recognising fractions which are several parts of a whole*
Shaded fraction cards (PCMs 33, 34), fraction cards (PCMs 31, 32)
Spread out the cards face up, keeping the fraction cards separate from the shaded fraction cards. The children take turns to find a matching pair of cards and place them together. The children check each other's pairs. They continue until all the cards are paired.

ACTIVITY 4
3-4 children

• *Recognising and creating fractions which are several parts of a whole*
Interlocking cubes in two colours, fraction cards (PCMs 31, 32)
Shuffle the fraction cards and place them in a pile face down. Each child takes a card, and demonstrates the fraction with the two colours of cubes. For example, if the selected card is $\frac{3}{5}$, they take five cubes of which three are one colour and two another. The children look at each other's cubes to check that they match the fraction. They then replace the cards. Repeat several times.

ACTIVITY 5
2-4 children

• *Recognising and creating fractions which are several parts of a whole*
Number cards (1 to 12) (PCMs 10, 11), squared paper, a fraction board (PCM 29)
Shuffle the cards, spread them out face down and select two of them. Place the smaller number above the larger number on the fraction board to show a fraction. The children colour a shape on their squared paper to match the fraction, e.g. if the fraction is $\frac{3}{5}$, they colour three squares in a 1 × 5 grid. The children check each other's shapes. Repeat the activity several times, creating different fractions.

Fractions/decimals

ACTIVITY 1
Whole class, in pairs

• *Recognising sets of equivalent fractions*
Squared paper (large squares)
The children draw and colour fraction walls. They illustrate halves, quarters and eighths by colouring in strips of squares, eight squares long. They can use these to demonstrate pairs of equivalent fractions, e.g. $\frac{2}{8} = \frac{1}{4}$. The children can draw a similar fraction wall on strips 12 squares long to illustrate thirds, quarters, sixths and twelfths.

ACTIVITY 2
2-3 children

• *Creating a pair of equivalent fractions*
Squared paper
The children draw a 1×5 grid and a 2×5 grid on their squared paper. They shade a fraction on their 1×5 grid, e.g. $\frac{3}{5}$, then shade a matching fraction of the 2×5 grid, e.g. $\frac{6}{10}$. They write the pair of equivalent fractions underneath, i.e. '$\frac{3}{5} = \frac{6}{10}$'. They repeat the activity to show fractions equivalent to $\frac{1}{5}$, $\frac{2}{5}$, $\frac{4}{5}$ and $\frac{5}{5}$. Repeat the activity using a 1×4 and a 2×4 grid.

ACTIVITY 3
2-4 children

• *Recognising sets of equivalent fractions*
Fraction cards (PCMs 31, 32)
The children sort the fraction cards into matching (equivalent) sets. They find how many equivalent sets there are, and how many fractions are in each set. They write the matching fractions, e.g. '$\frac{3}{4} = \frac{6}{8}$'. *Are there any fraction cards which have no other matching card?*

ACTIVITY 4
2-4 children

• *Recognising pairs of equivalent fractions*
Shaded fraction cards (PCMs 33, 34), fraction cards (PCMs 31, 32)
The children shuffle the shaded fraction cards and deal them out. Place the fraction cards in a pile, face down, and reveal the top card. The children take turns to match the fraction card with a card from their hand. The first child to find a matching pair places the two cards in front of them. When all the cards have been paired in this way, see who has the most pairs. Repeat several times.

ACTIVITY 5
2-4 children

• *Recognising pairs of equivalent fractions*
Shaded fraction cards (PCMs 33, 34)
The children sort the shaded fraction cards into matching (equivalent) sets. They find how many matching sets there are, and how many fractions in each set. They then write the matching fractions, e.g. '$\frac{1}{4} = \frac{2}{8}$'.

ACTIVITY 6
2-3 children

• *Creating pairs of equivalent fractions*
Equivalent fraction board (PCM 30), number cards (1 to 12) (PCMs 10, 11)
The children create pairs of equivalent fractions by placing the number cards on the equivalent fraction board. They investigate how many different pairs they can create when one fraction contains card number 1. How many others can they create?

ACTIVITY 7
1-2 children

• *Recognising equivalent fractions*
KidPix software (or similar drawing package)
Prepare a list of fractions, including some equivalent ones. Using Kidpix, the children draw rectangles and colour parts of them to represent the fractions. They should label the rectangles and position those for equivalent fractions next to each other.

N14 Addition/subtraction

ACTIVITY 1
Whole class, in five teams

- *Adding near multiples of 10 to a 3-digit number*
Three large dice
Give each team a near multiple of ten as their number. E.g. Team A has 29. One team throws the three dice together and creates a 3-digit number. Choose a child in that team to add their team number to the number created by the dice. They write the answer on the board. If they are correct they may add the two digits of the number and score the total. E.g. Team A throws the dice and obtains a 6, a 5 and a 2. They create 526 and add 29. The chosen child writes '555' on the board. The team therefore scores 5 + 5 + 5 which is 15. Continue until all the teams have had at least one turn each.

ACTIVITY 2
3 children

- *Adding near multiples of 10 to a 3-digit number*
Place-value cards (hundreds, tens, units) (PCMs 1 to 3)
Shuffle each set of place-value cards separately and place them in three piles face down. The children take turns to play. One child takes one card from each pile and creates a 3-digit number. They then add or subtract 29, 39 or 49 to their number and write the calculation. E.g. they create 367 and decide to add 39, and write '367 + 39 = 406'. Their score is the difference between their answer and the nearest multiple of 100. In this case their score would be 4. They continue until all the cards have been used.

ACTIVITY 3
3 children

- *Adding near multiples of 10 to a 2-digit number*
Number grid (1 to 100) (PCM 19), counters, a dice
One child throws the dice and moves a counter along their grid, starting at 1. They add 19 to the number they land on and write the addition. The children continue, taking turns to roll the dice. Whoever lands closest to 100 without going over it, is the winner. Repeat the activity, adding 29 instead of 19.

ACTIVITY 4
Pairs

- *Adding near multiples of 10 to a 3-digit number*
Three dice
The children take turns to throw three dice together and create a 3-digit number. Their partner has to partition that number into an addition pair of two 3-digit numbers, one of which must end in 9. E.g. the first child makes 641 and the second child partitions that number into 502 and 139. If they do this successfully, they write the addition and keep the first 3-digit number as their score. Repeat the activity several times with the children swapping roles.

ACTIVITY 1
Whole class, in pairs

- *Adding multiples of 1000*

Large thousands number cards (1000 to 9000)

Each pair writes down three thousands numbers between 5000 and 15 000. Ask a child to pick two cards. The children must add the numbers and write the addition. If any pair has written down that number they can cross it off. Replace the cards. Continue until one pair has crossed off three numbers.

ACTIVITY 2
3 children

- *Adding multiples of 10*

Place-value cards (hundreds, tens) (PCMs 1 to 3), a dice

Shuffle the cards separately and place them face down in two piles. One child turns over one card from each pile. They combine these to make a 2-digit multiple of ten. E.g. they take 200 and 50, and make 250. The second child throws the dice and writes that many tens, e.g. they throw a 4 and write '40'. The third child adds the two numbers, and writes the addition, e.g. '250 + 40 = 290'. The others check the addition. If it is correct, the third child adds the digits of the total to obtain their score, e.g. 2 + 9 + 0 = 11. Repeat several times with the children changing roles.

ACTIVITY 3
Pairs

- *Adding multiples of 10*

Coins (ten £1s, 15 or 16 10ps), a feely bag

Each child takes a handful of coins from the bag. They each work out how much they have and write the amount, e.g. '£3·20'. They then work out the amount in pence and write that, e.g. '320p'. They then calculate how much they will have if they combine their two amounts and write

the addition, e.g. '320p + 290p = 610p'. They combine their two sets of coins and check the total number of pence. *How much is this in pounds?* i.e. £6·10. Repeat several times.

ACTIVITY 4
3 children

- *Adding multiples of 100*

Place-value cards (hundreds) (PCMs 2, 3)

The cards are shuffled and spread out face down. One child turns over two cards. They add them together and write the addition. They score five if the other two children agree that the addition is correct. They then replace the cards and mix them up. Repeat several times with the children changing roles. Continue until one child has scored 30.

ACTIVITY 5
Pairs

- *Adding multiples of 100*

Working together, the children start with 100, add 200, then add 300, then add 400, etc. Before starting, they have to guess how many steps it will take them to get over 1000. How many steps will they need to get over 10 000? Then they work it out to see how close their guesses are.

N16 Place-value

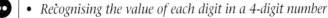

ACTIVITY 1
Whole class, in pairs

- *Recognising the value of each digit in a 4-digit number*
- *Recognising 1, 10, 100, or 1000 more/less than a 4- digit number*

Number cards (0 to 9) (PCM 10), a place-value board (thousands, hundreds, tens, units) (PCM 23)

Say a 4-digit number, e.g. *Three thousand, six hundred and fifty-eight.* Using the number cards, the children create the number on their place-value board, i.e. 3658. Repeat several times, with variations, e.g. ask the children to create the number which is 1 more; 1 less; 10 more; 10 less; 100 more; 100 less, 1000 more; or 1000 less than the number you say.

ACTIVITY 2
3-4 children

- *Reciting 3- and 4-digit numbers in sequence in ones*

Base Ten equipment (thousands, hundreds, tens, units)

The children create any 3-digit number using the Base Ten equipment, e.g. 352. They take turns to add a unit cube, and say the new number: *Three hundred and fifty-three, three hundred and fifty-four,* and so on. They exchange ten units for a ten when necessary. Repeat, starting with a 4-digit number.

ACTIVITY 3
3-4 children

- *Recognising 1, 10, 100, or 1000 more/less than a 4-digit number*

Place-value cards (thousands, hundreds, tens, units) (PCMs 1 to 5)

Give the children a target to aim for, such as '100 more than ....'. One child creates a 4-digit number with the place-value cards, e.g. 4732. All the children write the number which is 100 more, i.e. '4832'. Each child then reads their number, while the others check that it is correct. Repeat several times with the children swapping roles. Then give the children another target, such as '1000 less than ...'.

ACTIVITY 4
2 pairs

- *Recognising 1, 10, 100, or 1000 more/less than a 4- digit number*

Place-value cards (thousands, hundreds, tens, units) (PCMs 1 to 5), counters

Give the children a target to aim for, such as '10 less than ...'. One pair secretly creates a 4-digit number with the place-value cards, and reads it to the other pair, e.g. *Seven thousand, six hundred and fifty-two.* The other pair must write the number which is 10 less, i.e. '7642'. If they are correct, they collect a counter. Continue with the children reversing roles, and changing the number to be added or subtracted. Who collects the most counters?

ACTIVITY 5
3 children

- *Writing 4-digit number sequences in ascending and descending order*

A 1-minute timer

Decide on a sequence 'jump', e.g. counting forwards in 100s. The first child chooses a 4-digit starting number, e.g. 5631, sets the timer and says *Go!* The other two children each write the starting number and underneath it as many numbers as they can in ascending order, i.e. '5631, 5731, 5831, ...'. They stop after one minute. Look at the lists. How many mistakes are there? Are the numbers written correctly? Are there any missing? The children repeat the activity, taking different roles. Ask them to do the activity again, this time writing the numbers in descending order.

ACTIVITY 6
Pairs

- *Recognising 10 less than a 4-digit number*

Spreadsheet software

Prepare a spreadsheet file using the formula '=A1–10 ...' in Column B. The children take turns to say a 4-digit number, to which their partner gives the number 10 less. They enter the original number in Column A and check the answer in Column B. Extend the activity to finding 100 or 1000 less by altering the formula in the spreadsheet.

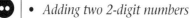

ACTIVITY 1
Whole class, in pairs

• *Adding two 2-digit numbers*
Large number cards (10 to 99)
Each pair writes down a 2-digit target number between 50 and 150. Ask a child to pick two cards and to show them to the class. Each pair must add the numbers and write the addition. If the total comes within ten of any pair's target number, the pair scores two points. If they hit their target number, they score ten points. Repeat several times.

ACTIVITY 2
3 children

• *Adding three 2-digit numbers*
Place-value cards (tens, units) (PCMs 1 to 3)
Shuffle the cards separately and place them face down in two piles. Each child takes one card from each pile. They lay them out and create three 2-digit numbers. Each child then adds the three numbers mentally, writes their total on a small piece of paper and folds it over so the others can't see. The children then work together to find the correct answer. They combine the tens cards and work out the total number of tens. They then combine the units cards and adjust the total number of tens accordingly, if necessary. When they agree on a correct answer, each child then unfolds their piece of paper. *Who was correct?* Can those who were incorrect see what they did wrong? The children replace the cards at the bottom of the piles and repeat the activity.

ACTIVITY 3
3 children

• *Adding three 2-digit numbers*
Number cards (10 to 99) (PCMs 10 to 16)
Shuffle the cards and place them in a pile face down. Each child takes a card and places it face up in front of them. They look at the tens and add them up, e.g. 40 + 50 + 30 = 120. One child writes the total. They then add the units, e.g. 8 + 5 + 9 = 23. Another child writes that total. The third child adds the two totals, e.g. 120 + 23 = 143. The children agree the total and write the complete addition, e.g. '48 + 55 + 39 = 143'. The cards are replaced at the bottom of the pile and the activity is repeated.

ACTIVITY 4
Pairs

• *Adding two 2-digit numbers*
Place-value cards (units, tens, except 70, 80, 90) (PCMs 1 to 3), number grid (1 to 100) (PCM 19), post-it notes
Shuffle the cards separately and place them face down in two piles. Each child takes a card from each pile and they create two 2-digit numbers. They discuss which number is the larger. One child points to that number on the grid. The other child must point at the tens in the smaller number. The first child then moves their finger down that many number of rows to add the matching number of tens. E.g. if the children pick cards 53 and 42, the first child puts their finger on 53 and the second child asks them to move their finger down four tens to 93. The second child then points at the units on the smaller number, and the first child moves their finger that many units along on the grid. E.g. they move their finger along from 93 to 95. The children then write the total on a post-it note, put the four cards in a pile and stick the post-it note on the top. Repeat the activity several times.

ACTIVITY 5
Pairs

• *Adding four 2-digit numbers*
Ask the children to find as many sets as possible of four 2-digit numbers which add to 60. Can they be sure that they have them all?

(N18) Addition/subtraction

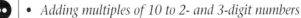

ACTIVITY 1
Whole class, in five teams

• *Adding multiples of 10 to 2- and 3-digit numbers*
Place-value cards (hundreds, tens) (PCMs 1 to 3), three dice
Shuffle the cards separately and put them in two piles face down. Choose a target number between 500 and 1000, which must be a multiple of 100, and write it on the board. Ask a child to take a card from each pile and create a 3-digit number with them, e.g. 400 and 50 makes 450. Write this number on the board. Each team throws the three dice together and creates a 3-digit number, e.g. Team A throws 3, 3 and 4 and creates 433. A child from each team then adds the two numbers, i.e. 450 + 433 = 883. The teams score ten points if their total has the same hundreds digit as the target number. Repeat the activity several times.

ACTIVITY 2
3 children

• *Adding three 3-digit multiples of 10*
Coins (15 £1s, 15 10ps), a feely bag
Each child takes a handful of coins and writes down the amount of money in pence. The children then compare the amounts. They each work out the total of the three amounts and compare their answers. They then check the total amount of money by combining their coins and counting how much they have. They then write the addition sentence. They replace the coins in the bag and repeat the process.

ACTIVITY 3
3 children

• *Adding three multiples of 100*
Number grid (1 to 100) (PCM 19), a dice, post-it notes, a calculator
Each child throws the dice twice and creates a 4-digit multiple of a hundred. E.g. they throw a 3 and a 5 and create 3500. They write each number on a post-it note. They discuss how to add the three numbers. (Covering the last two zeros can help the children focus on the best strategy, and they can use the 1 to 100 grid to help.) They add the three numbers and write the answer on a post-it note. The children then use the calculator to check their addition. Were they correct? If not, why not? If they weren't correct, they write the correct number below their original answer and lay out all the post-it notes together. Repeat several times.

ACTIVITY 4
Pairs

• *Adding a multiple of 100 to a 3-digit number*
Place-value cards (hundreds, tens, units) (PCMs 1 to 3)
Shuffle the cards separately and place them in three piles face down. One child takes a card from each pile and creates a 3-digit number, e.g. 300 and 60 and 7, making 367. The other child writes a multiple of 100, e.g. '400'. They then have to work out what the total of the two numbers is by adding the number of hundreds written by the second child to the hundreds number card. They write the addition, i.e. '367 + 400 = 767'. They leave the addition with the cards and start again, taking three more cards.

ACTIVITY 5
Pairs

• *Adding 4-, 3- and 2-digit numbers*
Number cards (0 to 9) (PCM 10)
The children use some or all of the cards to create an addition which has a total of 10 000. No number in the addition must be less than 100, e.g. 9876 + 124. How many ways can they find of doing this?

 **Addition/subtraction**

ACTIVITY 1
Whole class, in pairs

• *Mentally subtracting 2-digit numbers*
Place-value cards (tens, units) (PCMs 1 to 3)
Shuffle the cards separately and put them in two piles face down. Each pair writes down four numbers, one between 10 and 30, one between 30 and 50, one between 50 and 70, and one between 70 and 90. Take two cards, one from each pile. Show the children the 2-digit number. Each pair has to decide which of their numbers it is closest to. They then work out the difference between the two numbers. E.g. the children write down '24, 43, 55, 71' and you show them 67. Their number 71 is closest to this. They work out that the difference between 67 and 71 is 4. *Which pair has a difference which is closest to 10?* That pair scores one point. Repeat several times.

ACTIVITY 2
Pairs

• *Subtracting 2-digit numbers*
Coins (15 1ps, 15 10ps), a feely bag
Each child takes a handful of coins and works out how much they have, e.g. 47p and 32p. *Who has more money?* They work out the difference between the amounts by counting on from the smaller to the larger amount. *How much to the next 10p? How much to the larger amount?* E.g. 32p + 8p = 40p, then 40p + 7p = 47p. That is 8p and 7p, which makes 15p in total. The children write the subtraction and replace the coins. They repeat the activity until they have written ten different subtractions.

ACTIVITY 3
3 children

• *Subtracting 2-digit numbers*
Number line (1 to 100) (PCM 9), counters
The first child places a counter on the number line, and the second child has to place a counter in the next but one decade above that number. E.g. the first child places a counter on 34 and the second child places a second counter between 50 an 60. The third child then writes the subtraction, e.g. '52 – 34 = '. The children work out the difference using the number line: 34 to 40 is 6, and then 40 to 52 is 12; 6 + 12 = 18. They then complete the subtraction, e.g. '52 – 34 = 18'. The children remove the counters and start again, taking different roles.

ACTIVITY 4
Pairs

• *Subtracting 2-digit numbers*
Number line (1 to 50) (PCM 9), a dice, counters
Each child places a counter on number 1 on the number line. The children take turns to throw the dice and move their counter along the line. They have to calculate the difference between their position on the line and their partner's position and write a matching subtraction. E.g. I am on 12 and you are on 8. I write '12 – 8 = 4'. They continue moving along the line and calculating the difference each time. When each child reaches or passes 50, they add up all the differences, i.e. all the answers to their subtractions. The child with the largest score wins.

ACTIVITY 5
Pairs

• *Adding 4-, 3- and 2-digit numbers*
Number cards (0 to 9) (PCM 10)
Ask the children to try to find as many ways as possible of using the number cards to create subtractions with a difference of 9, e.g. 67 – 58 and 103 – 94 use all the cards except 2. *Can you find a set of subtractions with answers of 9 which uses them all?*

N20 Addition/subtraction

ACTIVITY 1
Whole class, in pairs

- *Mentally subtracting 2-digit numbers*
Large number cards (30 to 70)
Each pair writes down two numbers between 1 and 50. Turn over a card and show the children. Each pair has to choose one of their numbers and work out the difference between that number and the card number. They write down the subtractions. Choose two or three pairs to demonstrate their subtraction on the board. Each pair then adds the digits of their answer to find their score. Play several times and ask the children to keep a running total of their scores. Who has the largest score at the end?

ACTIVITY 2
Pairs

- *Subtracting 2-digit numbers*
Each child writes a list of ten 2-digit numbers between 20 and 90. Each child then chooses one of the numbers. Together they have to work out the difference between their two chosen numbers and write the matching subtraction. They then choose another number each and repeat the process. They continue until they have written ten subtractions.

ACTIVITY 3
Pairs

- *Subtracting 2-digit numbers*
Number grid (1 to 100) (PCM 19), a dice, counters
The children take turns to throw a dice. They each place a counter on the grid on a number beginning or ending in the dice number. They have to work out the difference between their two numbers and write a matching subtraction. They then throw the dice again and place two more counters on the grid. Continue playing until the children have written ten subtractions.

ACTIVITY 4
Pairs

- *Subtracting 2-digit numbers*
Blank 5 × 5 grid (PCM 26) filled in with 2-digit numbers at random
Each child chooses a number on the grid. They work out the difference between their two chosen numbers and write the matching subtraction. They repeat this ten times, choosing different combinations of numbers each time.

ACTIVITY 1
Whole class, in pairs

- *Counting on or back in 2s, 3s, 4s, 5s and 10s*
Large dice (2, 3, 4, 5, 10, red dot)
Each pair writes down a single-digit number. Throw the dice and, as a class, ask the children to count in steps of the number thrown. If you throw the red dot, the children can choose the size of the step. Write the numbers on the board as the children count. Ask the children to look at the numbers on the board. If the units digits include a number that a pair has written down, they score one point. Continue playing like this. Which pair has the highest score after several rounds? Discuss why this is.

ACTIVITY 2
Pairs

- *Counting on or back in 2s, 3s, 4s, 5s, and 10s*
Number cards (2, 3, 4, 5, 10) (PCM 10), a timer
One child starts the timer. The other child turns over a card and starts writing numbers in steps of the card number, starting at that number. How many numbers can they write before the timer runs out? The children swap roles and repeat the activity. They then swap their lists of numbers and check each other's count. The child who wrote the most numbers scores one point. Repeat the activity several times.

ACTIVITY 3
3 children

- *Counting back in 3s, 4s or 5s*
10 division number lines (PCM 20)
The first child writes 40 at the right-hand end of the number line. Counting in 4s, the second child writes in the next division of the line the number that comes before 40. Then the third child writes the number before that, and the first child writes the number before that. They continue until the line is complete. They repeat the activity, starting with 30 and counting back in 3s, then starting with 50 and counting back in 5s. Make the task more difficult by asking them to start at 80 and count back in 4s, or start at 90 and count back in 3s.

ACTIVITY 4
3 children

- *Counting in 3s and 4s*
Number line (1 to 50) (PCM 9), small stickers in three colours
Each child chooses a colour of sticker. One child chooses to count in 3s, one in 4s and one in 5s. They take turns to put one of their stickers on the number line on the first number in their count. They continue taking turns until they reach the end of the line. Some of the positions will have more than one sticker. Point out that they must be sure that they are on the correct space before they secure the sticker. Do they know why some spaces have more than one sticker?

ACTIVITY 5
Pairs

- *Recognising multiples of 2, 3, 4 and 5*
Number cards (0 to 9) (PCM 10)
Ask the children to write a list of numbers, counting in 4s from 4 to 100. Now let them do the same for the 3s and the 5s. Ask them to look at the 4s, choose one of the larger numbers and halve it. *Is the answer even or odd?* Repeat this several times. What do you notice? Now ask them to look at the 3s, choose one of the larger numbers and add the digits. Repeat this several times. *What do you notice?* Ask one child to write a 3-digit number. Can the others say if it would be in the 4s count, the 3s count or the 5s count? *How can you tell?* Repeat several times with the other children writing a 3-digit number.

N22 Multiplication/division

ACTIVITY 1
Whole class, in pairs

• *Multiplying by 6*
Number cards (1 to 10) (PCM 10), ×6 table list (PCM 24)
Shuffle the cards and place them face down in a pile. The children take turns to reveal a card, e.g. 5, and give that number of sixes, i.e. *Five sixes are thirty*. They check by recalling five threes, then doubling the result. They also check by chanting the multiples of 6 and by using the ×6 table. Repeat several times.

ACTIVITY 2
2-3 children

• *Creating the ×6 multiplication table*
2 cm-squared paper
On the 2 cm-squared paper, the children write '1, 2, 3, 4, 5, 6' along the first row of squares, then '7, 8, 9, 10, 11, 12' along the second row, and so on. They then write the multiplication table, writing '1 × 6 = 6' beside the first row, '2 × 6 = 12' beside the second row, etc, to complete the table.

ACTIVITY 3
3-4 children

• *Multiplying by 6*
Blank 5 × 5 grid (PCM 26) filled in with 1-digit numbers at random, blank 5 × 5 grid (PCM 26), a calculator
The children work together to multiply each grid number by 6, and record the answers in the matching spaces on the blank grid. They can recall ×3 facts, then double these if necessary. They then check their grid numbers with a calculator.

ACTIVITY 4
3-4 children

• *Recalling the ×6 multiplication facts*
Multiplication cards ×6 (PCM 36), interlocking cubes (in towers of 6), counters
Shuffle the cards and place them face down in a pile. The children take turns to reveal a card, read it out and then write the complete multiplication. They can use towers of six cubes to check. If they are correct, they take a counter. They check each other's answers. When all the cards have been used, start again.

ACTIVITY 5
2-3 children

• *Linking ×6 facts to ÷6 facts*
Multiplication and division cards (×6 , ÷6) (PCMs 36, 40), ×6 table list (PCM 24)
Shuffle the multiplication cards and place them in a pile face down. Spread out the division cards face up. The children take turns to reveal a multiplication card and say the answer. They then look for the matching division card. They can use the table list to check. If correct, they take both cards. Finally, they place all the cards in ascending order, matching multiplications and divisions. Repeat.

ACTIVITY 6
3-4 children

• *Linking ÷6 facts to multiples of 6*
Number cards (1 to 60) (PCMs 10 to 14), a dice, counters (in 3/4 colours)
Set out the cards in order to form a number line. Each child places a counter on card 1. They take turns to throw the dice and move a matching number of cards. If they land on a number in the ×6 table, they leave the counter there, and say the matching division, e.g. *Thirty divided by six is five*. On their next turn they use a new counter. At the end, the winner is the child with the most counters on the line.

ACTIVITY 7
2-4 children

• *Dividing by 6 with remainders*
Number cards (10 to 60) (PCMs 10 to 14), ×6 table list (PCM 24)
Each child is given a card which they keep secret. They divide the number on their card by 6, and write the complete division, including any remainders. Each card is then passed to the right, and the children do the same again. Continue until all the children have received each card. They then check each other's answers. They can use the ×6 table list as a check. Repeat with different cards.

N23 Multiplication/division

ACTIVITY 1
Whole class, in pairs

- *Multiplying by 9*
Number cards (1 to 10) (PCM 10), ×9 table list (PCM 24)
Shuffle the cards and place them face down in a pile. The children take turns to reveal a card, e.g. 4, and give that number of nines, i.e. *Four nines are thirty-six*. They check by using their fingers and chanting the multiples of 9. Finally, they check using the ×9 multiplication table. Repeat several times.

ACTIVITY 2
2-3 children

- *Creating the ×9 multiplication table*
2 cm-squared paper
Using the 2 cm-squared paper, the children write '1, 2, 3, 4, 5, 6, 7, 8, 9' along the first row, then '10, 11, 12, 13, 14, 15, 16, 17, 18' along the second row, and so on. They then write the ×9 multiplication table, writing '1 × 9 = 9' beside the first row, '2 × 9 = 18' beside the second row etc, to complete the table.

ACTIVITY 3
3-4 children

- *Multiplying by 9*
Blank 5 × 5 grid (PCM 26) filled in with 1-digit numbers at random, blank 5 × 5 grid (PCM 26), a calculator
The children work together multiplying each grid number by 9, and recording the answers in the matching spaces on the blank grid. They can use their fingers, if necessary, to help them. They can also use a calculator to check.

ACTIVITY 4
3-4 children

- *Recalling the ×9 multiplication facts*
Multiplication cards (×9) (PCM 38), interlocking cubes (in towers of 9), counters
Shuffle the cards and place them face down in a pile. The children take turns to reveal a card, read it out and then write the complete multiplication. They can use the towers of nine cubes to check. If correct, they take a counter. They check each other's answers. Continue until all the cards have been used. Repeat.

ACTIVITY 5
2-3 children

- *Linking ×9 facts to ÷9 facts*
Multiplication and division cards (×9, ÷9) (PCMs 38, 42), ×9 table list (PCM 24)
Shuffle the multiplication cards and place them in a pile, face down. Spread out the division cards face up. The children take turns to reveal a multiplication card and say the answer. They then look for the matching division card. They can use the ×9 table list to check. If correct, they take both cards. Finally, they place all the cards in ascending order, matching the multiplications and divisions. Repeat.

ACTIVITY 6
3-4 children

- *Linking ÷9 facts to multiples of 9*
Number grid (1 to 100) (PCM 19), a dice, counters (in 3/4 colours)
Each child places a counter on 1 on the number grid. They take turns to throw the dice and move a matching number of spaces. If they land on a number in the ×9 table, they leave the counter there, and say the matching division, e.g. *Forty-five divided by nine is five*. On their next turn they use a new counter. When they all reach 100, the winner is the child with the most counters on the grid.

ACTIVITY 7
2-4 children

- *Recognising number patterns involving multiples of 9*
Number cards (0 to 9) (PCM 10)
The children take two cards, make a 2-digit number, e.g. 74 and write it down. They reverse the cards and make another 2-digit number, i.e. 47, and write this down. The children then find the difference between the two numbers: 47 + 3 is 50, 50 + 24 is 74, therefore the difference is 27 (3 + 24). The children repeat the activity several times. What do they notice about all the differences?

N24 # Multiplication/division

ACTIVITY 1
Whole class, in pairs

• *Multiplying by 7*
Number cards (1 to 10) (PCM 10), ×7 table list (PCM 24)
Shuffle the cards and place them face down in a pile. The children take turns to
reveal a card, e.g. 3, and give that number of sevens, i.e. *Three sevens are twenty-
one.* They check by chanting the multiples of 7 and by using the ×7 table. Repeat.

ACTIVITY 2
2-3 children

• *Creating the ×7 multiplication table*
2 cm-squared paper
Using the 2 cm-squared paper, the children write '1, 2, 3, 4, 5, 6, 7' along the
first row, then '8, 9, 10, 11, 12, 13, 14' along the second row, and so on up to 70.
They then write, '$1 \times 7 = 7, 2 \times 7 = 14, ...$' beside the rows, to complete the table.

ACTIVITY 3
3-4 children

• *Multiplying by 7*
**Blank 5 × 5 grid (PCM 26) filled with 1-digit numbers at random, blank 5 × 5
grid (PCM 26), a calculator**
The children multiply each grid number by 7, and record the answers on the blank
grid. They can chant the multiples of 7 to help and use a calculator to check.

ACTIVITY 4
3-4 children

• *Recalling the ×7 multiplication facts*
Multiplication cards (×7) (PCMs 36, 37), cubes (in towers of 7), counters
Shuffle the cards and place them face down in a pile. The children take turns to
reveal a card, read it out and then write the complete multiplication. They can
use towers of seven cubes to check. If they are correct, they take a counter. They
check each other's answers. When all the cards have been used, start again.

ACTIVITY 5
2-3 children

• *Linking ×7 facts to ÷7 facts*
**Multiplication and division cards (×7, ÷7) (PCMs 36, 37, 39, 40), ×7 table list
(PCM 24)**
Shuffle the multiplication cards and place them in a pile face down. Spread out
the division cards face up. The children take turns to reveal a multiplication card
and say the answer. They then look for the matching division card. They can use
the ×7 table list to check. If correct, they take both cards. Finally, they place all
the cards in ascending order, matching the multiplications and divisions. Repeat.

ACTIVITY 6
3-4 children

• *Linking ÷7 facts to multiples of 7*
Number cards (1 to 70) (PCMs 10 to 15), a dice, counters (in 3/4 colours)
Place the cards in order to form a number line. Each child places a counter on
card 1. They take turns to throw the dice and move a matching number of cards.
If they land on a number in the ×7 table, they say the matching division, e.g.
Twenty-eight divided by seven is four, and leave the counter there, using a new counter
on their next turn. At the end, the child with the most counters on the line wins.

ACTIVITY 7
2-4 children

• *Dividing by 7 with remainders*
Number cards (10 to 70) (PCMs 10 to 15), ×7 table list (PCM 24)
Give each child a card to keep secret. They divide the card number by 7 and
write the complete division, including any remainder. Each card is then passed
to the right, and the children do the same again. Continue until all the children
have received each card. The children then check each other's answers. They can
use the ×7 table list to help them. Give them different cards and repeat.

ACTIVITY 8
2-3 children

• *Recalling multiplication facts*
Game 4: 'First to Three', two sets of number cards (1 to 10) (PCM 10), counters
(See instructions on the card.)

N25 Multiplication/division

ACTIVITY 1
Whole class, in pairs

- *Multiplying a number between 10 and 40 by 10 and 100*
Number cards (1 to 9) (PCM 10), place-value board (PCM 23)
Shuffle the cards and place them in a pile face down. Each child takes a turn to select two cards and makes a 2-digit number between 10 and 40, e.g. 23, by placing the cards in the tens and units positions on the place-value board. They then multiply their numbers by 10 by sliding the digits one place to the left, and by 100 by sliding them a further one place to the left. They write down both the resulting multiplications, i.e. '23 × 10 = 230, 23 × 100 = 2300'. Repeat several times.

ACTIVITY 2
2-3 children

- *Multiplying 1-digit numbers by 10*
- *Multiplying 1-digit numbers by 100*
Place-value cards (hundreds, tens, units) (PCM 1 to 3)
Shuffle the hundreds, tens and units cards separately and place them in three piles face down. The children take a units card, e.g. 7, and then find its matching tens card, i.e. 70. They place the units card on top of the tens card, and slide it to the left to show that 7 multiplied by 10 becomes 70. They record the multiplication '7 × 10 = 70'. Repeat several times then extend the activity to multiplying by 100. The children take a units card, e.g. 3, find the matching hundreds card i.e. 300, and record '3 × 100 = 300'. They should represent the multiplication by sliding the 3 card two places to the left. Repeat several times.

ACTIVITY 3
3-4 children

- *Dividing 3- and 4-digit multiples of 10 by 10 and by 100*
A calculator
One child uses the calculator and keys in a 3-digit multiple of 10, e.g. 260. Each of the other children divide this number by 10 and write down their division. The child with the calculator then checks the answer. Repeat several times, with the children taking turns to use the calculator. Extend to use 4-digit multiples of 100, e.g. 7400, which the children divide by both 10 and 100.

ACTIVITY 4
3-4 children

- *Multiplying a 2-digit number by 10 and by 100*
Number cards (10 to 100) (PCMs 10 to 16)
Shuffle the cards and place them in a pile face down. The first child decides whether to multiply by 10 or by 100 and tells the others his choice. He then takes a card and, keeping it hidden from the other children, multiplies the number by 10 or 100, as decided. He writes down the answer and shows it to the other children, who work out the number on the card. The first child shows them the card to check if they are correct. Repeat several times with the children taking turns to choose a card.

ACTIVITY 5
2 children

- *Multiplying 3- and 4-digit numbers by 10*
Number cards (1 to 9) (PCM 10), place-value board (PCM 23)
Shuffle the cards. One child deals out three cards to make a 3-digit number, e.g. 472. The other child multiplies the number by 10 and says the answer, i.e. *Four thousand seven hundred and two*. The first child checks the answer by sliding the cards along the place-value board. Repeat several times, taking turns to deal the cards. Extend the activity by using 4-digit numbers and by multiplying by 100.

Multiplication/division

ACTIVITY 1
Whole class, in pairs

• *Multiplying a 2-digit number by a 1-digit number*
Large number cards (10 to 30)
Choose a mutiplier, e.g. 3. Shuffle the cards and show one of them to the class, e.g. 24. Ask the children to multiply 3 by 24. One child in each pair is responsible for multiplying the tens, i.e. 3×20, and the other for multiplying the units, i.e. 3×4. Each pair then adds their two numbers to obtain the answer. Discuss the answers with the class. Each pair with a correct answer collects one point. Repeat for different numbers, with the children swapping the multiplication of the tens and units.

ACTIVITY 2
2-3 children

• *Multiplying a 2-digit multiple of 10 by a 1-digit number*
Place-value cards (10, 20, 30, 40, 50 and 1 to 9) (PCMs 1 to 3), Base Ten material (hundreds, tens)
Shuffle the cards separately and place them in two piles face down. The children choose one card from each pile to make a multiplication, e.g. 6×30. They take six lots of 30 in Base Ten, i.e. six lots of three tens. They put this together and change any sets of ten tens for 100 to give the answer, i.e. 180. They write down the complete multiplication, '$6 \times 30 = 180$'. Replace the cards and repeat several times.

ACTIVITY 3
3-4 children

• *Multiplying a 2-digit number by a 1-digit number*
Coins (£1, 10p, 1p), number cards (1 to 9) (PCM 10)
One child takes a handful of coins, e.g. 34p. Another takes a number card, e.g. 5. They put these together to form a multiplication, i.e. $5 \times 34p$. Each child writes down the calculation by splitting the 2-digit number into tens (30p) and units (4p), multiplying each part separately, then combining the two amounts. The children check the answers with the coins, taking five lots of 30p and five lots of 4p, and changing ten 10p coins for £1 if necessary. Repeat the activity with different children selecting the money and cards.

ACTIVITY 4
3-4 children

• *Multiplying a 2-digit number by a 1-digit number*
Number cards (1 to 9) (PCM 10)
The children choose a 2-digit number, e.g. 37, and create the ×37 multiplication table. They start by writing out each multiplication without the answers, e.g. '$1 \times 37 = ..$, $2 \times 37 = ..$', and so on. The number cards are shuffled, placed face down in a pile, and turned over one at a time, e.g. 7. Each child calculates 37×7 using the rectangle method, checks each other's answers, and completes the entry in the table. Continue until the table is complete. Repeat for a different 2-digit number.

ACTIVITY 5
2-3 children

• *Multiplying a 3-digit number by a 1-digit number*
Place-value cards (hundreds, tens, units) (PCMs 1 to 3), a dice, a calculator
Using the cards, the children create a 3-digit number between 100 and 200. They roll the dice to obtain a multiplier and then write the multiplication, e.g. '147×5'. The children then split the number into hundreds, tens and units, multiply each value by 5 and then combine the answers. They check each other's answers and use a calculator as a final check. Repeat several times.

ACTIVITY 1
Whole class, in pairs

- *Locating the position of fractions on a number line*

Blank fraction lines (PCM 28)

The children mark the end of each line with 0 and 1. They label any three fraction positions on each line. Point out to them that the lines are divided in the following order: thirds, quarters, fifths, sixths, eighths, tenths and twelfths.

ACTIVITY 2
2-3 children

- *Locating the position of fractions on a number line*
- *Beginning to order fractions*

Blank fraction lines (PCM 28)

Starting with a number line divided into quarters, the children label each point on the line, i.e. '0, $\frac{1}{4}$, $\frac{2}{4}$, $\frac{3}{4}$, 1'. They then write the list of fractions, in order. They then do the same on different fraction lines, e.g. fifths, tenths.

ACTIVITY 3
2-4 children

- *Locating the position of fractions on a number line*
- *Ordering two fractions*

Fraction cards (PCMs 31, 32), blank fraction lines (PCM 28), counters

Shuffle the cards and place them in a pile face down. The children take turns to draw two cards and decide which fraction is smaller. They can use the fraction number lines to check, by locating the position of each, and deciding which is closer to zero. The children check each other's answers. If they are correct, they take a counter and replace the cards at the bottom of the pile. Continue taking turns until one child has collected six counters.

ACTIVITY 4
2-4 children

- *Locating the position of fractions on a number line*
- *Stating a fraction smaller than a given fraction*

Fraction cards (PCMs 31, 32), blank fraction lines (PCM 28)

Shuffle the fraction cards and place them in a pile face down. The children take turns to reveal a card, and say a fraction which is smaller. Using the fraction number lines to help, the children check each other's answers. If they are correct, they keep the card; if not, they replace it. Introduce the rule that when the children say a fraction, it cannot have the same denominator as the one on the card. Who has collected the most cards? Alter the activity by asking the children to say which is the larger fraction.

ACTIVITY 5
2 pairs

- *Locating the position of fractions on a number line*
- *Ordering a set of fractions*

Fraction cards (PCMs 31, 32), blank fraction lines (PCM 28)

Deal out five cards to each pair. Each pair places the cards in a line, in order, from smallest to largest. They can use the fraction number lines to check. If they have two equivalent fractions, they place one above the other. The children check each other's ordering for any mistakes. Replace the cards, reshuffle, and play again. Vary the activity by changing the number of cards dealt out.

N28 Fractions/decimals

ACTIVITY 1
Whole class, in pairs

• *Finding fractions of amounts*
Interlocking cubes
Give each pair 12 cubes. Say a fraction, e.g. *One third*. The children have to show you one third of their cubes. Encourage them to divide the cubes into three equal parts. Discuss their answers. Ask a child to write '$\frac{1}{3}$ of 12 = 4' on the board. Repeat the activity several times and extend it by progressing from fractions with unit numerators, e.g. $\frac{1}{4}$, $\frac{1}{6}$ to fractions with non-unit numerators, e.g. $\frac{3}{4}$, $\frac{2}{3}$, $\frac{5}{6}$. You can also change the number of starting cubes to 20, for example.

ACTIVITY 2
2-3 children

• *Finding fractions (unit numerators) of amounts*
1p coins
The children take an even number of coins, e.g. 6p, and find one half of this amount by dividing it into two equal parts. They write their findings: '$\frac{1}{2}$ of 6p = 3p'. Repeat several times and then ask them to progress to thirds, quarters and eighths, dividing the coins into equal amounts each time, and recording the fraction of the amount.

ACTIVITY 3
2-4 children

• *Finding fractions of amounts*
Fraction cards (with denominators 2, 4, 8) (PCMs 31, 32), counters
Shuffle the fraction cards and place them in a pile face down. Take 16 counters and put them in a 2 × 8 arrangement. The children take turns to reveal a card, e.g. $\frac{3}{4}$, and take a matching number of counters, i.e. $\frac{3}{4}$ of 16 = 12 counters. The other children check the amount taken and if it is correct, the child who turned over the card keeps the counters. The children put new counters in the arrangement and another child has a turn. The children continue until all the cards have been taken. Who has collected the most counters?

ACTIVITY 4
2-4 children

• *Finding fractions of amounts*
Fraction cards (excluding denominators 5, 10) (PCMs 31, 32), 1p coins, counters
Shuffle the fraction cards and place them in a pile face down. Each child starts with 24p. The children take turns to reveal a card, e.g. $\frac{2}{3}$, and take a matching fraction of the 24 coins from their pile, i.e. 18. The children check each other's answers. The child who has taken the most 1p coins in that round collects a counter. Repeat several times, each time starting with 24 coins. The winner is the child who collects the most counters.

ACTIVITY 5
2-3 children

• *Finding different fractions of different amounts which have the same answer*
1p coins
The children use the coins to find different fraction statements which have the same answer. For example, if they choose 4p, this could be written as '$\frac{1}{2}$ of 8p, $\frac{1}{3}$ of 12p, $\frac{2}{3}$ of 6p, $\frac{4}{5}$ of 5p', and so on. Ask them to find four statements for each chosen amount. They can use the coins to help check their statements. Repeat for different amounts.

ACTIVITY 1
Whole class, in pairs

• *Rounding a 3-digit number to its nearest ten, and nearest hundred*
Number cards (0 to 9) (PCM 10)
Select three cards to create a 3-digit number. Choose a pair to say its nearest 100. Choose another pair to say its nearest 10. The rest of the class checks the answers. Rearrange the cards to make a different 3-digit number, and choose other pairs. When all possible 3-digit numbers have been made with the three cards and their nearest 10 and 100 have been announced, replace them with three different numbers and repeat.

ACTIVITY 2
2-3 children

• *Rounding a 3-digit number to its nearest ten*
A 20-division number line (PCM 20), a pointer
The children label one end of the line '240' and the other '260'. One child points to a position on the line, e.g. 252. The other children have to read the position, and say its nearest ten, i.e. *Two hundred and fifty-two: two hundred and fifty.* The children repeat the activity several times, sharing the roles. Repeat, labelling the number line with different numbers.

ACTIVITY 3
3 children

• *Rounding a 3-digit number to its nearest ten and nearest hundred*
Number cards (0 to 9) (PCM 10)
Shuffle the cards and place them face down in a pile. One child selects three cards and creates a 3-digit number, e.g. 491. The next child says the nearest hundred, i.e. *Five hundred.* The third child says the nearest ten, i.e. *Four hundred and ninety.* The children then write down the numbers, '491 – 500, 491 – 490'. They repeat the activity several times, taking turns to create the 3-digit number.

ACTIVITY 4
2-4 children

• *Estimating an amount of money by looking at coins*
Coins (£1, 10p and 1p), a feely bag
Place the coins in the bag. One child takes a large handful of coins, and places them on the table. Each child estimates how much money is in the pile, and writes an estimate both to the nearest pound (100p) and nearest 10p. The children then sort the coins, and find out exactly how much is in the pile. They round the amount to its nearest pound and nearest 10p. *Was anyone's estimate exactly right?* The children replace the coins and repeat the activity, taking turns to collect the money.

ACTIVITY 5
2-4 children

• *Rounding a 4-digit number to its nearest ten, hundred and nearest thousand*
Two sets of number cards (0 to 9) (PCM 10), counters
The children shuffle the cards and lay out five 4-digit numbers in a row. They take turns, moving along the row, to say a number to its nearest thousand. They then do the same for its nearest hundred, and finally for its nearest ten. They check what each other is saying, and give a counter for each correct number. *Who has collected the most counters?* The children reshuffle the cards and play again.

ACTIVITY 6
4 children

• *Rounding a 2-digit number to its nearest ten*
Game 5: 'The Nearest Ten', two sets of number cards (2 to 6) (PCM 10), cubes
(See instructions on the card.)

N30 Addition/subtraction

ACTIVITY 1
Whole class, in pairs

- *Adding 3-digit numbers*
A large dice
Each pair writes down a 3-digit number. Throw the dice three times and create a 3-digit number. Each pair adds this number to their number. Any pair whose answer makes either a set of consecutive numbers or is the same three digits scores five points. Repeat several times and continue until one pair has 20 points.

ACTIVITY 2
3 children

- *Adding 3-digit numbers*
Number grid (10 to 1000) (PCM 27), place-value cards (hundreds, tens, units) (PCMs 1 to 3)
Shuffle the cards separately and place them in three piles face down. The children take turns to choose a 3-digit number from the grid. They each take one card from each pile and arrange them to make a second 3-digit number. They then add the two 3-digit numbers together. The children then check each other's additions. They repeat the activity until all the numbers on the grid have been used twice.

ACTIVITY 3
3 children

- *Adding 3-digit numbers*
Tell the children that they are to create a palindrome – a number which reads the same forwards as backwards. They start with a 3-digit number, reverse the digits and then add the two numbers. They repeat this as many times as necessary until they obtain a palindrome. E.g. 251 + 152 = 403, 403 + 304 = 707. (The process can be quite lengthy.)

ACTIVITY 4
3 children

- *Adding 3-digit numbers*
Place-value cards (hundreds, tens, units) (PCMs 1 to 3), a dice
The cards are shuffled separately and placed face down in three piles. The children decide which of them will work with either the hundreds, the tens or the units. They each throw the dice to decide the number of their hundreds, tens and units. Together they create their 3-digit number and write it down, e.g. 462. They then take a hundreds and a tens card and arrange them to make a 3-digit number, e.g. 470. Remembering which value they are working with, the children now add the two numbers, first by adding the units together, e.g. 0 + 2 = 2, then the tens, e.g. 13 tens or 130, and finally the hundreds, not forgetting any hundreds calculated by the child in charge of the tens. The children write down the total, e.g. 932. They then check that they are correct. Repeat several times.

ACTIVITY 5
Pairs

- *Adding 3-digit numbers*
Number cards (1 to 9) (PCM 10)
The children arrange the cards so that they have three 3-digit numbers. They then add the numbers together and write the total. Can they make the total as near as possible to 1000?

ACTIVITY 1
Whole class, in pairs

• *Subtracting 3-digit numbers*
Tens cards (50 to 300) (PCMs 13 to 18)
Write a target number on the board, e.g. '536'. Each pair writes a number between the target number and 1000. Give each pair a card. Each pair subtracts their card number from the number they chose. The pair whose answer is nearest to the target number wins. Keep the same target number and let each pair keep their number. Give each pair a new card, and play again. Continue, changing the target number occasionally.

ACTIVITY 2
3 children

• *Subtracting 3-digit numbers*
Place-value cards (hundreds 600 to 900, tens 60 to 90, units) (PCMs 1 to 3), a dice
Shuffle the cards separately and place them in three piles face down. The children take one card from each pile and lay out the 3-digit number, e.g. 673. They throw the dice twice and create a 3-digit multiple of ten, e.g. 350. They then write a subtraction using their numbers, e.g. '673 – 350 =' . One child works out the subtraction and writes the answer. The other children then check the answer and discuss how they know if it is correct. The cards are then replaced and the activity repeated.

ACTIVITY 3
3 children

• *Subtracting 3-digit numbers*
Coins (1p, 10p, £1), a feely bag
One child takes some £1 coins, another takes some 10p coins and a third takes some 1p coins. They add up the total amount of money, put the coins in the bag and write down the total amount in pence, e.g. '347p' (three £1s, four 10ps, seven 1ps). The first child takes some £1 coins from the bag. The children work out how many pence they have taken, e.g. 200p or £2. Together, they calculate how much they have left in the bag, e.g. '347 – 200 =' . When they have agreed, they complete the subtraction, i.e. '347 – 200 = 147'. The children then check the amount in the bag to see if they were correct. They then empty the bag and repeat the activity.

ACTIVITY 4
Pairs

• *Subtracting 3-digit numbers*
Number cards (1 to 9) (PCM 10)
Write this subtraction on the board: 'abcd – efo = hgd'. Tell the children that each letter represents a digit. Given that o = 0, can they work out what the other letters represent?

N32 Addition/subtraction

ACTIVITY 1
Whole class, in pairs

- *Subtracting a 2-digit number from a 3-digit number*
Number cards (30 to 60) (PCMs 12 to 14) two dice
Give each pair a number card. Write '183' on the board. Each pair subtracts their card number from 183. They do this twice more. Throw the two dice together. Create two 2-digit numbers from the dice throw and write them on the board. Any pair with one of these numbers as their answer wins. Repeat several times.

ACTIVITY 2
3 children

- *Subtracting a 2-digit number from a 3-digit number*
One child writes a 3-digit number. The second child reverses the order of the digits. The children write the larger number first and create a subtraction, e.g. '742 – 247'. Taking the smaller number, the third child counts on to the nearest ten, writing down what they add, e.g. '3'. The first child counts on from there to the nearest hundred, writing down what they add, e.g. '50'. The second child counts on to the larger number, writing down what they add, e.g. '442'. The third child adds all three components, e.g. 3 + 50 + 442 = 495 and the children write the answer to the subtraction. Repeat the activity, starting with a different 3-digit number. What do the children notice about the middle digit in all their answers?

ACTIVITY 3
Pairs

- *Subtracting 2-digit numbers*
Number grid (1 to 100) (PCM 19), counters
One child puts a counter on the grid. The other child puts a counter on a number in a different row. The children write down both numbers, larger first, as a subtraction sentence, e.g. '64 – 37'. They use the number grid to help them count on from the smaller to the larger, e.g. 37 and 3 makes 40, and 20 makes 60 and 4 makes 64: 3 + 20 + 4 = 27. Continue until the children have written ten subtractions.

ACTIVITY 4
Pairs

- *Subtracting a 2-digit number from a 3-digit number*
Number cards (0 to 9) (PCM 10)
Ask the children to use the cards to create a subtraction where one 2-digit number is subtracted from one 3-digit number. They may only use each card once, e.g. 175 – 82 = 93. *How many different subtractions can you find?*

N33 Addition/subtraction

ACTIVITY 1
Whole class, in five teams

- *Subtracting a 3-digit number from a 3-digit number*
Place-value cards (hundreds, except 100, tens, units) (PCMs 1 to 3)
Shuffle the cards separately and place them in three piles face down. Give each team a card from each pile and ask them to create a 3-digit number. Write '139' on the board and ask each pair to subtract it from their 3-digit number. They should do this individually and then compare their answers before agreeing a final answer. Repeat this three times. Now write '333' on the board. *Which team has an answer which is closest to 333?* That team scores a point. Repeat several times.

ACTIVITY 2
3 children

- *Subtracting a 3-digit number from a 3-digit number*
Coins (1p, 10p, £1, at least nine of each)
Ask the children to make three different piles of money, each containing between 200p and 500p. The children write down the amount in each pile. They each concentrate on one of the amounts and subtract 129 from it. They then check their subtraction by removing 129p from each pile in turn, exchanging coins when necessary. Repeat the activity using different piles of money and subtracting a different amount, e.g. 143p.

ACTIVITY 3
3 children

- *Subtracting a 2-digit number from a 3-digit number*
Place-value cards (hundreds, tens, units) (PCMs 1 to 3), a dice, a calculator
The cards are shuffled separately and placed face down in three piles. The children take one card from each pile to create a 3-digit number. The first child then throws the dice and writes that many tens, e.g. they throw a 5 and write '50'. The second child then subtracts the multiple of ten from the 3-digit number and writes the answer. The third child uses the calculator to check the subtraction. Repeat several times with the children swapping roles.

ACTIVITY 4
Pairs

- *Subtracting a 3-digit number from a 3-digit number*
Number cards (1 to 9) (PCM 10)
Starting with 1000, ask the children to use the cards to create a 3-digit number to subtract from 1000. The children then take the answer as their starting number and repeat the process several times, using as many of the cards as possible, without using any of them more than once. Can the children use all the cards and finish with a single-digit number? *Can you find other ways of doing this?*

N34 Properties of number

ACTIVITY 1
Whole class, in pairs

- *Recognising odd and even numbers to 1000*
Place-value cards (hundreds, tens, units) (PCMs 1 to 3)
Shuffle the cards separately and place them in three piles face down. Each pair decides whether to collect even or odd numbers. They then decide on a hundreds digit, e.g. a pair could decide to collect even numbers beginning with 700. Take a card from each pile and create a 3-digit number. Show the children. *Can any pair claim this number?* If so, that pair scores five points. Replace the cards and continue playing.

ACTIVITY 2
3 children

- *Recognising odd and even numbers to 1000*
Coins (1p, 10p, £1, at least nine of each)
Each child takes a handful of one type of coin. The children combine their coins and work out the amount of money, writing it in pence, e.g. '638p'. They discuss the amount and decide whether it is even or odd. If it is even, they write 'even' beside the amount and return the coins to their piles. If it is odd, they must write the even numbers on either side of the amount. They then return the coins and play again.

ACTIVITY 3
3 children

- *Recognising patterns when adding odd and even numbers*
Ask the children to draw a 3 × 3 grid and write a 2-digit even number in each space. The children then add the numbers in each row and column. *What do you notice about the totals?* Ask them to repeat the activity, this time writing an odd number in each space. Again, the children should add the numbers in each row and column. *What do you notice about the totals this time?* Can the children explain why this occurs?

ACTIVITY 4
3 children

- *Recognising odd and even numbers to 100*
Number cards (50 to 100) (PCMs 13 to 16), card for labels ('odd', 'even')
Shuffle the number cards and place them face down in a pile. Each child takes a card and lays it in front of them. They have to say if it is even or odd, explaining why. The children then place the number card by the appropriate label. They continue until all the cards have been sorted. The children then line up the cards in the even set from smallest to largest and then do the same for the odd set.

ACTIVITY 5
Pairs

- *Recognising odd and even numbers to 1000*
Ask the children to explore the multiplication patterns of odd and even numbers. What happens when they multiply two even numbers together? What about two odd numbers? What about an odd number multiplied by an even number?

ACTIVITY 1
Whole class, in pairs

- *Counting forward and back from zero*
- *Recognising negative numbers*

Large number cards (0 to 9)
Shuffle the cards and place them in a pile face down. Each pair chooses three numbers between 10 and –10 and writes them down. Write a number between 5 and -5 on the board. Take a card and show it to the class. Tell the children that together you will count back from the number on the board in that number of single steps. E.g. you write '3' on the board and the card number is 6, so you count back, *Two, one, zero, negative one, negative two, negative three*. Write ' –3' on the board. If any pair has this number they may cross it out. Continue playing like this. The first pair to cross out all three of their numbers wins.

ACTIVITY 2
3 children

- *Counting forward and back from zero*
- *Recognising negative numbers*

A 3 × 3 magic square
Ask the children to draw a 3 × 3 blank grid. Taking turns, the first child chooses a number on the magic square and counts back ten. The children write the negative number they reach in the matching space on their blank grid. Continue until all the squares in the blank grid are filled in. Repeat the activity with a new blank grid, but this time count back 12 from the numbers in the magic square.

8	1	6
3	5	7
4	9	2

ACTIVITY 3
3 children

- *Counting forward and back from zero*
- *Recognising negative numbers*

A 10 division number line (PCM 20), a dice
The children mark the mid-point '0' on the blank number line. They fill in the positive and negative numbers to 5 and –5. Then they take turns to throw the dice. The child throwing the dice starts at any point on their line and counts back the number thrown by the dice. They write their starting number, the dice number and where they landed. Continue for several throws of the dice.

ACTIVITY 4
3 children

- *Counting forward and back from zero*
- *Recognising negative numbers*

Ask the children to work out how many numbers there are between 50 and –50 inclusive. *How many of these numbers contain a 9?*

N36 **Multiplication/division**

ACTIVITY 1
Whole class, in pairs

- *Doubling multiples of 10 and 100*
Two dice
Throw the two dice together and use the numbers thrown to create a multiple of 100, e.g. throw a 3 and a 4 to create the number 340. One child in each pair is responsible for doubling the hundreds, and the other for doubling the tens. Each pair then combines their two numbers to obtain their double. Discuss the answers with the class. Each pair with a correct answer collects one point. Repeat with the children alternating doubling the hundreds and tens.

ACTIVITY 2
3-4 children

- *Doubling multiples of 100*
Place-value cards (100, 200, 300, 400, 500) (PCM 2), Base Ten materials (hundreds, thousands)
Shuffle the cards and spread them out face down. The first child takes a card and collects a matching number of hundreds in Base Ten material. The second collects the same amount of material. The third child writes down the number and doubles it. The children count the total amount of material in both sets. Is the third child correct? The children continue, sharing the roles, until all the cards have been used.

ACTIVITY 3
3-4 children

- *Doubling 3-digit multiples of 10*
Place-value cards (hundreds, tens) (PCMs 1 to 3), coins (£1, 10p, 1p)
Shuffle the place-value cards separately and place them face down in three piles. The children take turns to choose one card from each pile to create a 3-digit number, e.g. 340. They try to say its double. They then take double that number of £1 coins and 10p coins, i.e. double three lots of £1 coins, and double four lots of 10p coins, to see if their answer is correct. If it is, the child keeps the cards. Continue until all the cards have gone. *Who collected the most cards?*

ACTIVITY 4
3-4 children

- *Halving even multiples of 100*
Place-value cards (thousands, even hundreds, even tens) (PCMs 1 to 5), coins (£1, 10p, 1p), counters
Shuffle the cards separately and place them face down in three piles. One child reveals a hundreds card and a tens card to make a 3-digit number, e.g. 480 and all the children attempt to write its half. Together they collect a matching number of pence, i.e. four £1 coins and eight 10p coins, and then divide them into two equal amounts, changing a £1 coin for ten 10p coins if necessary. They count each amount then check that this matches what they wrote down. Those who were correct collect a counter. Continue, with the children swapping roles, replacing the money and choosing different cards. *Who has collected the most counters?*

ACTIVITY 5
Pairs

- *Doubling 4-digit multiples of 100*
- *Halving 4-digit multiples of 100*
Each child chooses a 4-digit multiple of 100, e.g. 4700, and writes it down. They then calculate its double and write the answer on a separate sheet of paper which they swap with their partner. The children then halve the number which is written down. They then check that these halves match the first numbers that were chosen. If they don't match, the children must try to spot where they went wrong. Repeat with different numbers.

ACTIVITY 1
Whole class, in pairs

• *Multiplying a 2-digit number by a 1-digit number using a standard written method*
Large number cards (10 to 30)
Choose a multiplier, e.g. 3. Shuffle the cards and show one of them to the class, e.g. 18. Ask each pair to write down the calculation (3 × 18) vertically, and write an estimate above it. Discuss the estimates. Each pair then writes their calculation, making sure they agree. Discuss the answers. Each pair with a correct answer collects one point. Repeat for different multiplications.

ACTIVITY 2
2-3 children

• *Multiplying a 2-digit multiple of 10 by a 1-digit number*
Place-value cards (tens) (PCM 1), Base Ten material (hundreds, tens), a dice
Choose a place-value card at random, e.g. 60, and throw the dice, e.g. 4. Create a multiplication with these numbers, i.e. 60 × 4. The children try and work out the calculation mentally, relating four lots of 6 tens to four lots of 6. They then check their answer using the Base Ten material, taking four lots of sixty, and changing any sets of ten tens for 100 until they have the answer, i.e. 240. They write down the multiplication, '4 × 60 = 240'. Replace the cards and repeat several times.

ACTIVITY 3
3-4 children

• *Multiplying a 2-digit number by a 1-digit number, using a standard written method*
Coins (£1, 10p, 1p), number cards (1 to 9) (PCM 10)
One child takes a handful of coins, e.g. 46p. Another takes a number card, e.g. 7. These form a multiplication, i.e. 7 × 46p. Each child writes down the calculation with an estimate above it. The children then work out the answer with the help of the money, taking seven lots of 40p and seven lots of 6p, changing ten 10p coins for £1, if necessary. They then compare the answers with their estimates. Repeat several times with the children swapping roles.

ACTIVITY 4
3-4 children

• *Multiplying a 2-digit number by a 1-digit number, using a standard written method*
Number cards (1 to 10) (PCM 10)
The children choose a 2-digit number, e.g. 58, and create the ×58 multiplication table. They start by writing down each calculation without the answers, e.g. '1 × 58 = .., 2 × 58 = ..', and so on. The children shuffle the number cards and turn them over one at a time, e.g. 4. Each child calculates 4 × 58 using the standard written method, checks each other's answers, and completes the entry in the table. The children continue until the table is complete and then compile a different table.

ACTVITY 5
2-3 children

• *Multiplying a 3-digit number by a 1-digit number, using a standard written method*
Place-value cards (hundreds, tens, units) (PCMs 1 to 3), a dice, a calculator
Create a random 3-digit number between 100 and 200. Choose a mutiplier by throwing the dice. Write the multiplication on the board, e.g. '186 × 3'. The children split the number into hundreds, tens and units, multiply each value by 3, then combine their three answers, so that the written calculation has three sections. They check each other's answers and use a calculator as a final check. Repeat several times.

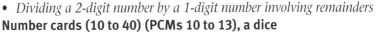 N38 Multiplication/division

ACTIVITY 1
Whole class, in threes

• *Dividing a 2-digit number by a 1-digit number involving remainders*
Number cards (10 to 40) (PCMs 10 to 13), a dice
Shuffle the cards and place them face down in a pile. The first child takes a card and reads the number aloud. The second child writes the number. The third child throws the dice and the second child writes this number. The children work together to divide the card number by the dice number, e.g. 32 ÷ 6 = 5 and 2 left over. If they throw a 1, they divide by 10. The children repeat the activity 12 times, sharing the roles.

ACTIVITY 2
2-3 children

• *Dividing a 2-digit number by a 1-digit number involving remainders*
Interlocking cubes
The children agree on a divisor, e.g. 4. They take a handful of cubes, e.g. 23, and make piles of four cubes. They count the number of piles, i.e. five, and see how many are left over, i.e. three. They then write down the complete division, i.e. '23 ÷ 4 = 5 r 3'. They replace the cubes, choose another divisor and repeat, writing the calculation each time.

ACTIVITY 3
3-4 children

• *Dividing a 2-digit number by a 1-digit number involving remainders*
Number cards (10 to 40) (PCMs 10 to 13), a dice, counters, interlocking cubes
Shuffle the cards and place them face up in a large circle. Each child places a counter on a card. They take turns to throw the dice and move around the circle. They divide the number thrown, e.g. 5, into the number of the card they are on, e.g. 34: 34 ÷ 5 is 6 remainder 4. They then take the number of the remainder in cubes, i.e. four cubes. Continue until one child has collected 20 cubes.

ACTIVITY 4
3-4 children

• *Dividing a 2-digit number by a 1-digit number involving remainders*
Game 6: 'Remainder Trail', a dice, interlocking cubes, counters
(See instructions on the card.)

ACTIVITY 5
2 pairs

• *Dividing a 2-digit number by a 1-digit number involving remainders*
Number cards (1 to 10) (PCM 10), two dice, 10p coins
Shuffle the cards and place them in a pile face down. Each child from one pair throws a dice to make a 2-digit number and writes it down, e.g. '62'. One child from the other pair turns over a card, e.g. 4, and the other child writes the division, i.e. '62 ÷ 4'. The children work out the answer together, taking any remainder number in 10p coins, i.e. 20p. The children continue, taking turns until one pair has collected £4.

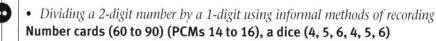

ACTIVITY 1
Whole class, in pairs

- *Dividing a 2-digit number by a 1-digit using informal methods of recording*
Number cards (60 to 90) (PCMs 14 to 16), a dice (4, 5, 6, 4, 5, 6)
Shuffle the cards and place them face down in a pile. One card is revealed, e.g. 84, and the dice is thrown to determine the divisor, e.g. 6. This creates the division: 84 ÷ 6. Each pair writes the division and records the number of sixes which make 84. They start by working out if there is enough for ten sixes, then seeing how many are left over. Check the answers together. Any pair with a correct answer collects one point. Repeat, several times.

ACTIVITY 2
2-3 children

- *Dividing a 2-digit multiple of 10 by a 1-digit number involving remainders*
Interlocking cubes
The children choose a number, e.g. 4, and write the answers to dividing all the multiples of 10 up to 100 by 4. As they do so, they create a division table, e.g. '10 ÷ 4 = 2 r 2, 20 ÷ 4 = 5', and so on. To help them with the divisions, they can use the interlocking cubes. Repeat the activity using a different divisor.

ACTIVITY 3
2 pairs

- *Dividing a 2-digit number by a 1-digit number using standard written methods of recording*
Number cards (70 to 100) (PCMs 15, 16), interlocking cubes, counters
Shuffle the cards and place them face up in a large circle. One of the children chooses a card, e.g. 84. Each pair calculates the result of dividing the card number by 3, then checks to see if they agree. They write down the division, using the standard method of recording. They can check their answer by using the interlocking cubes. If they are correct, they collect a counter. They then divide the same number by 4, then by 5, and so on up to 8. *Who has collected the most counters?* Repeat the activity, choosing a different number card.

ACTIVITY 4
4 children

- *Dividing a 2-digit number by a 1-digit number using standard written methods of recording*
Coins (10p, 1p)
One child takes a handful of coins, e.g. 63p. Each child calculates how much they will receive if the money is shared equally between the four of them. They record the calculation '63 ÷ 4 =' using the standard written method, including any remainders if necessary. They then check each other's answers. Finally, they divide the coins between them, changing a 10p coin for ten 1p coins, if necessary. They check that this amount matches the answers. They replace the coins, take a new handful, and repeat.

ACTIVITY 5
2-3 children

- *Dividing a number between 100 and 200 by a 1-digit number*
- *Estimating the result of a division*
A dice, a calculator
The children choose any number between 100 and 200, e.g. 134, then roll the dice to obtain a divisor, e.g. 5. This creates a division, i.e. 134 ÷ 5. Each child makes an estimate of the answer and writes it down. The children each calculate the division using the standard method, then check their answers. They make a final check using a calculator. Point out to them that the calculator produces its remainders in decimal form. Compare the results with the estimates.

N40 Fractions/decimals

ACTIVITY 1
Whole class, in pairs

• *Using decimal notation*
Base Ten equipment (flats as units, rods as tenths), a dice
Establish that the flats are units and the rods are tenths. The children take turns to throw the dice, and take a matching number of tenths. They write down how many tenths they have, e.g. *I took 4 tenths so I write '0·4'*. When they have collected ten tenths, they exchange them for a unit. Continue until someone has collected 4·0.

ACTIVITY 2
2-3 children

• *Using decimal notation*
Squared paper
Using the squared paper, the children draw strips of ten squares, and colour them to represent tenths of a number. They write the decimal number alongside the coloured squares, e.g. for 7 squares '0·7'. They extend this by colouring some whole strips and part of a strip to show for example, 2·4.

ACTIVITY 3
2 pairs

• *Recognising and using decimal notation (tenths)*
Place-value cards (units) (PCMs 2, 3), decimal place-value cards (tenths) (PCM 6) interlocking cubes
Shuffle the cards separately and place them face down in two piles. In pairs, the children take turns to pick two cards and create a decimal number. The other pair is allowed seven questions to help them guess what number they have created. e.g. *Are the units less than five? Is the decimal part less than a half?* If they are correct, they take a cube. The children continue, swapping roles, until all the cards have been used.

ACTIVITY 4
2-4 children

• *Recognising the position of decimal numbers on a number line*
• *Recognising the relationship between fractions and decimals*
10 division number lines (PCM 20)
The children label the end points of one number line '4' and '5'. They select four points along the line, labelling the points above the line as a fraction, e.g. '$4\frac{3}{10}$', and below the line as a decimal, e.g. '4·3'. Repeat the activity on new number lines, labelling the end points, for example, '7 and 8', '0 and 1', '10 and 11'.

ACTIVITY 5
2-4 children

• *Recognising the position of decimal numbers on a number line*
• *Recognising the relationship between fractions and decimals*
100 division number lines (PCM 20)
The children label the ends of one number line 0 and 10. They select eight points along the line, labelling each point above the line as a fraction, e.g. '$2\frac{7}{10}$', and below the line as a decimal, e.g. '2·7'. Repeat the activity, using more number lines and labelling the ends for example, '10 and 20', '90 and 100'.

ACTIVITY 1
Whole class, in pairs

• *Using decimal notation*
£10 in coins (£1, 10p, 1p), feely bag
A child from each pair takes a handful of coins and they both sort them out into £1, 10p and 1p coins. They write how much they have using decimal notation, e.g. '£3·52'. They then write the amount of change they would receive from £10, i.e. '£6·48'. They then check whether this is the amount left in the bag. Repeat the activity, with the other child taking the coins from the bag.

ACTIVITY 2
2-3 children

• *Using decimal notation*
Squared paper
Using the squared paper, the children draw a grid of 10×10 squares. Tell the children that each square in the grid represents one hundredth of a whole. The children colour in squares to represent numbers with hundredths. They write the decimal number alongside each section of colouring, e.g. for 73 squares '0·73'. They also write down the portion of the grid that is not coloured. They extend this to colouring in larger areas to show for example, 1·47.

ACTIVITY 3
2 pairs

• *Recognising and using decimal notation*
Place-value cards (units) (PCMs 2, 3), decimal place-value cards (hundredths, tenths) (PCMs 6 to 8), cubes
Shuffle the cards separately and place them face down in three piles. The children from one pair take turns to choose three cards and create a decimal number. The other pair is allowed eight questions to help them guess the number. e.g. *Is the number greater than five? Is the decimal part less than a quarter?* If they are correct, they take a cube. Continue, swapping roles, until all the cards have been taken.

ACTIVITY 4
2-4 children

• *Positioning decimals on a number line*
• *Recognising the relationship between fractions and decimals*
100 division number lines (PCM 20)
The children label the end points of one number line 0 and 1. They select eight points along the line, labelling each point above the line as a fraction, '$\frac{37}{100}$', and below the line as a decimal, e.g. '0·37'. Repeat the activity, labelling the end points such as, '1 and 2', '5 and 6'.

ACTIVITY 5
2-4 children

• *Positioning decimals on a number line*
• *Recognising the relationship between fractions and decimals*
100 division number lines (PCM 20), decimal place-value cards (tenths, hundredths) (PCMs 6 to 8)
The children label the end points of one number line 0 and 1. Shuffle the cards separately and place them in two piles face down. The children take turns to select two cards from each pile to make two decimal numbers, e.g. 0·36 and 0·78. They then label these points on the line. They score the difference between the two numbers, i.e. 0·42. The winner of the round is the child with the largest difference. Replace the cards and play again.

ACTIVITY 6
2-3 children

• *Saying a decimal number in words*
Game 7: 'Thousandths to One', a dice, interlocking cubes
(See instructions on the card.)

Addition/subtraction

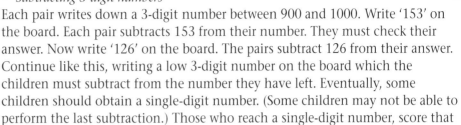

ACTIVITY 1
Whole class, in pairs

• *Subtracting 3-digit numbers*
Each pair writes down a 3-digit number between 900 and 1000. Write '153' on the board. Each pair subtracts 153 from their number. They must check their answer. Now write '126' on the board. The pairs subtract 126 from their answer. Continue like this, writing a low 3-digit number on the board which the children must subtract from the number they have left. Eventually, some children should obtain a single-digit number. (Some children may not be able to perform the last subtraction.) Those who reach a single-digit number, score that number. Repeat, with you and the children starting with a different number.

ACTIVITY 2
3 children

• *Subtracting 3-digit numbers*
Number cards (0 to 9) (PCM 10)
Shuffle the cards and place them face down in a pile. Each child takes a card. They put them together to make the largest number possible and each write down this number. They then rearrange the cards to make the smallest number possible which they also write down. The children then each subtract the smaller number from the larger. They compare their answers and agree which is correct. The children then replace the cards and start again. Continue like this until the children have done at least five subtractions.

ACTIVITY 3
3 children

• *Subtracting 3-digit numbers*
Place-value cards (hundreds, tens, units) (PCMs 1 to 3), a dice
Shuffle the cards separately and place them face down in three piles. The children take one card from each pile. They put these together to make a 3-digit number, e.g. 635. The first child then throws the dice and writes that multiple of 100, if it is smaller than their 3-digit number, or that multiple of ten, if it is not. E.g. they throw 4 and write 400. The second child subtracts 400 (or 40) from their number. The others each check the calculation. The children all write the subtraction. They then replace the cards and repeat the activity, swapping roles.

ACTIVITY 1
Whole class, in pairs

• *Subtracting decimals in the form of money*
A dice
Each pair chooses an amount between £5 and £10 and writes it down. Throw the dice three times and create an amount of money using the dice numbers. Write the amount on the board. Each pair must subtract this amount from their amount. Check their additions. Any pair who has an amount with the same number of pounds as pence may score 10p. Repeat several times until one pair has accumulated 50p.

ACTIVITY 2
Pairs

• *Subtracting decimals in the form of money*
Coins (1p, 10p, £1, at least ten of each)
Each child takes an amount between £5 and £10 in coins and writes it down. The children compare their amounts and work out the difference. They should write the subtraction and calculate the answer, and then check by comparing the actual coins. The children replace the coins and repeat the activity six times, writing each subtraction.

ACTIVITY 3
3 children

• *Subtracting decimals in the form of money*
Coins (1p, 10p, £1, at least ten of each)
One child takes an amount between £2 and £5 in coins and writes it down. The second child removes the 10p coins. They then write how much is left. The third child removes the 1p coins and writes the amount left. The children look at the three amounts and check that they correspond with the coins removed. Repeat several times.

ACTIVITY 4
Pairs

• *Subtracting decimals in the form of money*
Ask the children how many pairs of amounts of money they can write which have a difference of less than £1 and a sum of exactly £10.

M1 Length

ACTIVITY 1
Whole class, in pairs

- *Selecting a suitable unit of measurement: mm, cm, m, km or miles*

Write the following list on the board:

1. The distance from here to New York
2. The length of my thumb
3. The length of the video box
4. The length of a racing car
5. The height of a church tower
6. The length of a spider's leg
7. The height of a double-decker bus
8. The width of a butterfly's wings
9. The depth of a village pond
10. The distance from the earth to the moon

Ask the children to discuss, in pairs, which unit of measurement they would choose to measure each of the suggestions listed and to write them down. When they have all agreed on the units, discuss as a class the list and the children's choices.

ACTIVITY 2
4 children

- *Estimating and measuring in m and cm*

A metre rule (calibrated in cm), counters

Ask the children to choose an object which is more than one metre long. They each estimate its length and write their estimate in metres and centimetres. The children then measure the actual length of the object using the rule and write down the measurement. They then find and write the difference between the actual length and their estimates. The children record their results on a table:

	Estimate	Length	Difference
Rug	1 m 40 cm	1 m 65 cm	25 cm

The child whose estimate is closest collects a counter. Repeat several times.

ACTIVITY 3
4 children

- *Estimating and measuring in m and cm*

A metre rule or tape measure (calibrated in cm)

The children measure each other's reach, that is, the distance from the arm pit to the tip of the finger, when the arm is outstretched. They record their measurements in centimetres. Repeat, measuring other body measurements.

ACTIVITY 4
4 children

- *Estimating and measuring in m and cm*

A metre rule (calibrated in cm), string, scissors

The children measure around different objects, such as their head, their wrist, a ball, etc. They wrap string around the objects, mark the length on the string, remove the string and cut it. They then extend the string along the metre rule to find the actual measurement and write the lengths of the string in centimetres.

ACTIVITY 5
Pairs

- *Estimating and measuring in m and cm*

A metre rule (calibrated in cm)

Ask the children to find three long, thin objects. They order them from shortest to longest and then hold the longest one against the metre rule, taking care to ensure that it is lined up with the edge of the rule. They record how long it is in centimetres. The children then write down estimates of the lengths of the two shorter objects. Then they measure each one using the rule.

ACTIVITY 6
Pairs

- *Estimating the number of km from the number of miles*

A local map or road atlas

The children find two places on the map. They work out how far apart they are in miles. They then estimate how far this would be in kilometres. They record the places and the distances and repeat the activity, choosing two different locations.

M2 Weight

ACTIVITY 1
Whole class, in pairs

- *Estimating weights, using a suitable unit*

Sugar in a paper cup, a slipper, a woolly hat, a book, a cushion, a teddy bear, a mug, a clock, a school bag, weighing scales, weights in grams

Hold up each item in turn. Ask the children to discuss in their pairs how much they think the items weigh in grams and to write down their estimates. Then use the scales to weigh each item separately. How close are the children's estimates to the actual weights? The children score five points if they are within 100 g of the actual weight, and ten points if they are closer than 50 g. Who gains the highest score?

ACTIVITY 2
2-3 children

- *Estimating and weighing objects in grams*

Objects weighing less than 1 kg, ten 100 g weights, a balance

The children choose one of the objects and feel how heavy it is. They estimate and write its weight in hundreds of grams. They then weigh the object, to the nearest 100 g, counting how many weights are just too much and how many are not quite enough to balance the object. They write down the actual weights to the nearest 100 g and compare them to their estimates.

ACTIVITY 3
2-3 children

- *Estimating and weighing objects in kilograms*

Six objects weighing more than 1 kg, several 1 kg weights, ten 100 g weights, a balance

The children feel the weight of each object and discuss which they think is the heaviest and which is the lightest. They arrange the objects in order of estimated weight and record the order. They weigh each object separately to the nearest 100 g, using kilogram and 100 g weights. They record the weight of each item in kilograms and grams, and also in grams only. E.g. the dictionary weighs 1400 grams or 1 kg 400 g. Was their initial ordering of the objects correct?

ACTIVITY 4
2-3 children

- *Working out individual weights from weighing a collection*

Sets of identical objects, weights (10 g, 20 g, 50 g and 100 g), a balance

The children choose a set of identical objects, e.g. wooden bricks, place a 100 g weight on one side of the balance and find out how many bricks are needed to balance the weight. They record the result, e.g. 100 g = 20 bricks. They then do a rough calculation to find out how much each brick weighs. Then they use the lighter weights to weigh one brick and to find out how close their estimate is. The children record their findings. They repeat the activity for different sets of objects.

ACTIVITY 5
2-3 children

- *Calculating weights of different objects using weighing and comparisons*

Bags containing 150 g, 200 g, 250 g, 300 g of sugar, a 50 g weight, a 100 g weight, a balance, post-it notes

Using only the weights provided, the children order the bags of sugar from heaviest to lightest and find out how much each one weighs by comparing the different bags and weights on the balance.

Capacity

ACTIVITY 1
Whole class, in pairs

• *Estimating capacities, using a suitable unit*
An empty fizzy drink can, a pint bottle, a mug, an eggcup, a dessert spoon, a vase, a litre measure (calibrated in 100 millilitres), lentils
Hold up each item in turn. In their pairs, the children discuss each item, and estimate its capacity in litres. Then measure the capacity of each one by filling it with lentils and pouring them into the litre measure to find how many millilitres of lentils each one holds. How close were each pair's estimates?

ACTIVITY 2
3 children

• *Estimating and measuring capacity, using a suitable unit*
A litre measure (calibrated in 100 millilitres), several containers with capacities of less than 1 litre, water
The children choose a container, estimate its capacity in hundreds of millilitres and record their estimate. They fill the container with water then pour the water into the litre measure, to find the capacity to the nearest 100 ml. They record their findings in a table.

	Estimate	Capacity
Vase	400 ml	nearly 500 ml

How close were their estimates? They replace the container and repeat the activity until they have measured each container.

ACTIVITY 3
3 children

• *Estimating and measuring capacity, using a suitable unit*
A litre measure (calibrated in 100 millilitres), containers with capacities of more than and less than 1 litre, water
The children discuss which container they think holds the least and which holds the most. They then arrange the containers in order of estimated capacity, from the least to the most and record the order. Using water and the litre measure, they then find the capacity of each container. They record the capacities in litres and millilitres. Was their order correct?

ACTIVITY 4
3 children

• *Estimating and measuring capacity*
A litre measure (calibrated in 100 millilitres), an eggcup, a 5 ml teaspoon, water
The children estimate how many 5 ml teaspoons of water an eggcup will hold. They then use the 5 ml teaspoon to fill the eggcup with water, counting how many teaspoons it takes. The children then estimate how many eggcups of water will fill the litre measure and record their estimate. They then use the eggcup to fill the litre measure, counting the number of eggcupfuls very carefully. How close was their estimate?

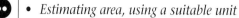 **Area**

ACTIVITY 1
Whole class, in pairs

• *Estimating area, using a suitable unit*
Used postcards, used stamps, cm-squared paper
Give each pair a postcard. Ask the children to estimate how many square centimetres the postcard will cover when it is stuck on the sheet of squared paper. Show the children the squared paper and ask them to write down their estimate. Give each pair some squared paper and encourage the children to draw round the postcard. They then count or calculate the number of square centimetres that the postcard covers. Each pair writes down the area of their postcard. They then work out the difference between the actual area of the postcard and their estimate. Repeat the activity estimating and calculating the area of a stamp.

ACTIVITY 2
4 children

• *Recognising that the area of a rectangle is length times width*
• *Introducing square centimetres as a measure*
A large piece of squared paper (or several smaller sheets stuck together)
Spread the paper out on the floor. Choose a child to lie on it, arms at their sides. The other children draw around him, and cut out the shape. They take one section each and find the area of their part of the shape, colouring squares as they go. Write the total area in the middle of the shape and display the picture on the wall.

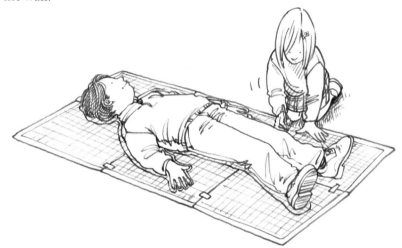

ACTIVITY 3
3-4 children

• *Recognising that the area of a rectangle is length times width*
• *Introducing square centimetres as a measure*
Squared paper, felt-tip pens
Ask the children to draw as many different shapes as they can with an area of six squares. All the squares must join on at least one side. How many different shapes can the children find?

ACTIVITY 4
3 children

• *Recognising that the area of a rectangle is length times width*
• *Introducing square centimetres as a measure*
Squared paper, felt-tip pens
The first child draws a row of four squares, and colours them. The second child draws a second row of four squares next to the first line and colours them. The third child draws a third row of four squares next to these and colours them. The first child draws a line around the whole rectangle. The children work together to calculate the area of the rectangle and write the answer, i.e. area = 12 squares. The children repeat the activity, sharing the roles and colouring in a row of five squares.

M5 Perimeter

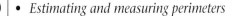

ACTIVITY 1
Whole class, in pairs

- *Estimating and measuring perimeters*
Video cassette boxes, string, metre rule (calibrated in cm), scissors, cm-squared paper
Each pair lays their cassette box on the table and carefully puts a length of string around the perimeter of the box. They cut the length of string and extend it along the rule, making sure that one end of the string is right at the end of the rule. They write down the length of the string. The children now draw around the video box on squared paper. They then measure the sides of the rectangle they have drawn and calculate the perimeter. How close was their string estimate to their calculation?

ACTIVITY 2
2+ children

- *Introducing the meaning of perimeter*
- *Consolidating differences between area and perimeter*
Cm-squared paper, scissors
The children draw and cut out different rectangles. They find the perimeters of the rectangles by counting the centimetres on the edges. They then find the areas of the rectangles either by counting the squares inside or multiplying length by width. They write the results inside the rectangles, e.g. 'P = 20 cm, A = 25 cm^2'.

ACTIVITY 3
2+ children

- *Introducing the meaning of perimeter*
Different small rectangles of paper or card (labelled A, B, C, ...), 30 cm rules (calibrated in cm)
The children find the perimeters of the rectangles by measuring the length and width of each. They record the results, e.g. 'A: length = 8 cm, width = 5 cm, perimeter = 26 cm'. They then arrange the rectangles in a line, from smallest perimeter to largest.

ACTIVITY 4
2+ children

- *Introducing the meaning of perimeter*
Cm-squared paper, five squares of the same size
The children take the five squares and join them edge to edge to make a shape. They copy the shape on the squared paper and write the perimeter beside it, e.g. 'P = 8 units'. Can the children make eight different shapes? Do they all have the same perimeter?

ACTIVITY 5
Pairs

- *Estimating and measuring the perimeter of a book*
Books, long strips of paper, metre rule (calibrated in cm), scissors
The children cut four strips of paper to the same length as each side of their chosen book. They then put their strips carefully end-to-end and stick them together, making sure that the strips do not overlap. They then use the metre rule to measure them. *How long is the joined strip? This is the distance all the way round your book.* The children write down the length of the book's perimeter in centimetres.

ACTIVITY 6
3+ children

- *Introducing the meaning of perimeter*
A metre rule
The children estimate and measure the perimeter of some large rectangles in the classroom or school. Examples include: the floor, the carpet, the hall floor, the blackboard. The children estimate the perimeters in metres and measure the sides to the nearest metre to find the perimeters. How close are their estimates?

Time

ACTIVITY 1
Whole class, in four teams

- *Telling the time to 5-minute intervals on analogue clocks*
- *Recognising a.m. and p.m. time*

A large analogue clock, a coin

Give each team a range of times, for instance, Team A: a.m. times in the half hours before each hour, e.g. 7:45 in the morning; Team B: a.m. times in the half hours after each hour, e.g. 7:15 in the morning; Team C: p.m. times in the half hours before each hour, e.g. 4:45 in the afternoon; and Team D: p.m. times in the half hours after each hour, e.g. 4:15 in the afternoon. Set the hands on the clock to a certain time. (The hour hand should be on a five-minute interval.) Toss the coin: heads is a.m., tails is p.m. Tell the children the time and say whether it is morning or afternoon/evening. E.g. *Quarter to five in the morning*. Give the team whose range includes this time five points. Ask that team what they might be doing at that time. Repeat several times.

ACTIVITY 2
6 children

- *Recognising and telling the time in 1-minute intervals*

Clock faces (one sheet per child) (PCM 43), number cards (1 to 59) (PCMs 10 to 14), felt-tip pens

Shuffle the cards and place them in a pile face down. The children work in pairs, Each child takes a card, e.g. 39, and draws the minute hand onto a clock face to indicate the number of minutes past the hour given on their card, i.e. twenty-one minutes to the hour. The children pass their work to their partner, who checks it to see if the time matches the card, and writes the digital time beside the clock face. They return their work to their partner for checking. They repeat the activity eight times.

ACTIVITY 3
2 pairs

- *Recognising and telling the time in 1-minute intervals*

Number cards (1 to 59) (PCMs 10 to 14), two sheets of paper divided in two and headed 'Past', 'To'

Shuffle the cards and spread them out face up. The pairs take turns to choose two cards that make 60, e.g. 37 and 23. They place each card in the appropriate part of their sheet of paper (37 'past' and 23 'to'). They continue until all the cards are taken.

ACTIVITY 4
3 children

- *Recognising and telling the time in 1-minute intervals*

A working analogue clock, a dice, Blu-tack

One child puts a piece of Blu-tack on the clock face where the tip of the minute hand is pointing to, e.g. 10:24 and says *Go!*. The second child throws the dice as many times as possible while the third writes down the running total, e.g. '5, 7, 13, 14, 15, 20, 24, ...' When they reach 100 the first child says *Stop!* and places a second piece of Blu-tack over the spot now marking the tip of the minute hand on the clock face, e.g. 10:42. The children write the times indicated by the Blu-tack, work out the number of minutes it took them to reach a score of 100, i.e. 18 minutes, and write this next to the start and finish times. The children repeat the activity several times, sharing the roles. What is the quickest time they achieve?

ACTIVITY 5
3 children

- *Recognising and telling the time*

Spreadsheet software

Prepare a spreadsheet file similar to the one shown. Use the 'If logical' function '=IF(C1="05:00";"correct";" ")' in Column D. The children read the times in Column A and enter the corresponding digital time in Column C. They check Column D to see if their answer is correct.

	A	B	C	D
1	5 o'clock	is the same as	05:00	correct
2	ten past seven	is the same as	07:10	correct
3	twenty-five to 9	is the same as		
4	12 minutes to 10	is the same as		

(M7) Time

ACTIVITY 1
Whole class, in pairs

- *Reading a calendar*

A copy of the current month's calendar

Give each pair a copy of the current month's calendar. They pick a day of the week and colour all the instances of that day on their calendar. Read out an event – either one that is planned for the current month or one that occurs regularly, e.g. Christmas Day. The children decide on which date the event occurs and then write it on their calendar. If the event occurs on their chosen day, the children score 7 points. Repeat, saying some events that occur each week and some that happen only once.

ACTIVITY 2
3-4 children

- *Reading a calendar*

A calendar (cut into months), a counter (one for each child), a dice, cubes

The children choose a month each and place their counters on the first day. They take turns to throw the dice and move along the month in date order. If they land on a Monday or a Friday, they take two cubes, if they land midweek, i.e. Tuesday, Wednesday or Thursday, they take one cube, and if they land on a weekend, i.e. Saturday or Sunday, they take three cubes. The children continue until they reach the end of the month. Who has the most cubes?

ACTIVITY 3
3 children

- *Reading a calendar*

Old calendars

The children cut up the calendars into separate months. They shuffle the months, then each take a turn to put them in order from January to December. How long do they each take?

ACTIVITY 4
3 children

- *Reading a calendar*

Number cards (1 to 31) (PCMs 10 to 12), a calendar, blank labels

The children make a set of 'day' labels, Monday to Sunday, and place these in order in front of them. Shuffle the number cards and place them face down in a pile. The children take turns to reveal a card, check the matching date on the calendar for the day of the week, then place the card beside its matching day in front of them. The winner is the first to collect a card for each day of the week.

ACTIVITY 5
3-4 children

- *Reading a calendar*

A calendar

The children investigate how many Mondays there are in each month. They record these, then find the total number of Mondays in a year. They repeat for each day of the week. Are all the totals the same?

ACTIVITY 1
Whole class, in pairs

• *Reading a timetable*
A copy of the class timetable
Give each pair a copy of the class timetable. They choose two lessons or events on it and shade them in. Look at the timetable and read out a day and a session. The children work out what happens on that day at that time. If that session is one that they shaded, they can shade another session as well. Repeat several times. Who has shaded the most of the timetable?

ACTIVITY 2
3 children

• *Understanding and reading a timetable*
Copies of weekly TV programme guides
The children look through the TV programme guide together and find two programmes each day for a week which they would all like to watch. They write their names, their starting times and the number of minutes each programme lasts. Which programme is the longest? Which is the shortest?

ACTIVITY 3
3 children

• *Understanding and reading a timetable*
Some small 'cards'
The children plan a timetable for a party together. They have to fit at least five of the following events into the party: tea, football, a disco, a video, hide and seek, musical bumps, pass-the-parcel, pinning the tail on a donkey, a puppet show, a conjuror, laser quest, a swim ... The children decide what time the party will start and end, the events there will be and their order, and how long each one will take. Finally, the children make some party invitations with a programme of events on them.

ACTIVITY 4
2 pairs

• *Understanding and reading a timetable*
Copies of weekly TV programme guides
Each pair looks at the programmes listed in the TV programme guide to find the cartoons. One pair tries to work out how many hours of cartoons there are on ITV each week, the other pair does the same for BBC1. Remember, some are 'hidden', i.e. they take place as part of another programme like 'Live and Kicking'. At the end, the children compare totals. The children repeat the activity for the news programmes – how many hours of news are there on BBC1 and on ITV?

Time

ACTIVITY 1
Whole class, in five teams

- *Measuring time in seconds*

A seconds timer

Choose a child from one team. Give the child an action to perform, e.g. jumping twenty times. Ask their team to estimate the time it will take them to complete this action. When the team has agreed an estimate, time the child performing the action. The team scores the number of seconds difference between the actual time and their estimate. Choose a child from another team and give them a different action, e.g. clapping forty times. Each team has two turns. Which team scores the least?

ACTIVITY 2
3 children

- *Measuring time in seconds*

A stop-clock, dominoes

Spread out the dominoes face up, randomly placed. One child is the timer and operates the stop-clock. The other two children get ready to sort the dominoes. When the timer says *Start*, she starts the clock and the other children find all the dominoes with six spots on. When they think they have finished, they say *Done* and the timer stops the clock. The timer checks to see if they are correct. If so, they score the number of seconds shown on the clock. If not, they score the number of seconds shown on the clock plus a penalty of ten for every domino they missed. The children repeat the activity, sharing the roles, finding all the dominoes with five spots on, then those with four, then three and so on. At the end, who has the lowest score?

ACTIVITY 3
2 pairs

- *Measuring time in seconds*

A stop-clock, a dice

One pair throws the dice, while the other pair times them, until they throw a 1. How long does it take? They swap roles, timing how long it takes to throw a 2, 3, 4, 5, 6. Which number takes longest?

ACTIVITY 4
5 children

- *Recognising that there are 60 seconds in 1 minute*

A 60-second timer

One pair does the timing, writing a list of the group's names and setting the clock for sixty seconds. The other three children close their eyes and try to estimate one minute exactly. They knock on the table when they think one minute has passed. The timers write the number of seconds that have passed when each child knocks. Who was closest? Each child is awarded a score of the difference between the number of seconds they indicated and sixty seconds. The player with the lowest score wins. The children repeat the activity, sharing the roles.

S1 2-d shape

ACTIVITY 1
Whole class, in pairs

- *Drawing and naming polygons*
A dice (3, 4, 5, 6, 7, 8), rulers
One child rolls the dice. Using rulers, each child
number of sides as the dice number. The children c
write the name of the polygon inside it. Repeat sev
different shapes can they draw?

ACTIVITY 2
2-3 children

- *Using the language of 2-d shape*
5 × 5 geoboards, elastic bands, geoboard shape paper (PCM 44)
The children create a polygon on their geoboard, then copy it by drawing its
shape on the geoboard paper. They write the name of the polygon underneath
the drawing. How many different shapes can they create and draw?

ACTIVITY 3
2 children

- *Recognising polygons*
- *Counting the number of sides of polygons*
Game 8: 'Side Track', a dice, counters, interlocking cubes
(See instructions on the card.)

ACTIVITY 4
Pairs

- *Using the language of 2-d shape*
Geoboards, elastic bands, geoboard shape paper (
The children sit back to back. One child makes a
describes it to their partner – the number of si
tries to make the same shape on their board,
children then compare their shapes and each
they the same? Repeat the activity several tir

ACTIVITY 5
2-4 children

- *Recognising and naming polygons*
Shape cards (PCM 45)
Shuffle the cards and place them in a pile, face dow
reveal a card and name the shape. The rest of the gr
correct. If they are, they keep the card; if not, th
have been turned over, who has the most? Reshuffle the cards a..
the children that they should use the name 'quadrilateral' for 4-sided shapes.

ACTIVITY 6
3-4 children

- *Drawing polygons using a Roamer*
**Roamer (pre-set to 5 cm units and right-angle turns), pen pack, large sheets of
paper**
The children enter a sequence of instructions into the Roamer to draw a square
(using a pen pack will give clear evidence of success). Then ask them to do the
same for a rectangle. As a variation, ask the children to input the instructions for
a square or rectangle, using the 'REPEAT' key.

ACTIVITY 7
3 children

- *Constructing polygons with right angles*
Geoboards, elastic bands, geoboard shape paper (PCM 44)
The children work together to make shapes on their geoboards. They try to make
shapes with different numbers of right-angles, e.g. a shape with 1 right-angle, 2
right-angles etc. Can they make a 3-sided, 4-sided, or 5-sided shape, each with 1
right-angle, with 2 right-angles, etc? They then record their shapes on the
geoboard paper, marking the right-angles in each shape.

S2 2-d shape

ACTIVITY 1
Whole class, in pairs

- *Drawing and naming regular polygons*
Plastic regular polygons
The children place a regular polygon on a sheet of paper and carefully draw round it. They write the name of the polygon beneath the shape, e.g. 'regular pentagon'. Continue until they have drawn a collection of different regular polygons.

ACTIVITY 2
2-3 children

- *Recognising and naming regular and irregular polygons*
Shape cards (PCM 45)
Shuffle the cards and place them face down in a pile. The children take turns to reveal a card and name it as either *regular* or *irregular*. They check each other's answers. If they are correct, they keep the card; if not, they replace it at the bottom of the pile. Continue until all the cards have been turned over. *Who has the most?*

ACTIVITY 3
2 children

- *Classifying triangles according to type*
Plastic triangles (isosceles, equilateral, right-angled), feely bag
The children place the triangles in the bag. They take turns to draw a triangle from the bag, say its type (*isosceles, equilateral, right-angled* or *other*), and describe why it is that particular type, e.g. *It is an isosceles triangle, because it has two equal sides.* The children check each other's descriptions

ACTIVITY 4
2-3 children

- *Recognising and naming regular and irregular polygons*
Plastic polygons (regular and irregular), blank cards
The children sort the polygons into two groups: regular and irregular. Using the blank cards, they write labels for each of the regular polygons, e.g. 'regular hexagon' and place them alongside each polygon. They then do the same for the irregular polygons, e.g. 'irregular heptagon'.

ACTIVITY 5
2-4 children

- *Creating and drawing isosceles triangles*
5 × 5 geoboards, elastic bands, geoboard shape paper (PCM 44)
The children create different isosceles triangles on their geoboards, then copy them onto the geoboard paper. How many different isosceles triangles can they find?

ACTIVITY 6
3-4 children

- *Drawing regular polygons*
LOGO software
This activity assumes that the children already know how to use LOGO. Give the children a record sheet (as shown). The children use the information given to draw a square, rectangle and triangle in LOGO. They then work out how to draw a regular pentagon and hexagon, and complete the table. Extend the activity by challenging the children to draw other polygons using the table as a hint.

shape	number of sides	turn at each corner	sides × turn
square	4	90°	360°
rectangle	4	90°	360°
triangle	3	120°	360°
pentagon	5		360°
hexagon	6		360°

ACTIVITY 1
Whole class, in pairs

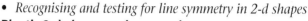

- *Recognising and testing for line symmetry in 2-d shapes*
Plastic 2-d shapes, scissors, rulers
The children choose a shape which they think is symmetrical. They carefully draw around the outline of the shape, then cut it out. They fold it to test for symmetry. If it is symmetrical, they draw over the fold line with a ruler, and mount the shape onto a backing sheet. How many symmetrical shapes can each pair find?

ACTIVITY 2
2-3 children

- *Creating symmetrical shapes by folding, drawing and cutting*
Coloured paper, scissors
The children fold the paper, then draw and cut out a shape around the fold line. They open it out to create a symmetrical shape, which they then mount onto a backing sheet. They create a range of different symmetrical shapes, experimenting with straight lines only, curved lines only, and a combination of the two.

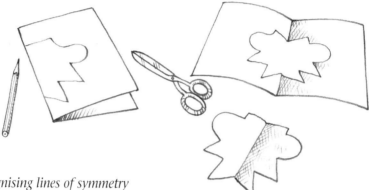

ACTIVITY 3
2-4 children

- *Recognising lines of symmetry*
Shape cards (PCM 45), small mirrors
The children draw a line of symmetry on any of the shapes which they think are symmetrical. They then explore for symmetry in the shapes, using a mirror. They label those shapes which are symmetrical.

ACTIVITY 4
2-3 children

- *Recognising shapes which have line symmetry*
Shape cards (PCM 45), small mirrors
The cards are shuffled and placed in a pile face down. The children take turns to reveal a card, and decide whether or not it is symmetrical. If they think it is symmetrical, they show where a line of symmetry is. After they have looked at the cards, they place them in a pile, according to whether they are symmetrical or not. The children check each other's answers, using a mirror if necessary. When all the cards have been sorted, reshuffle them and repeat the activity.

ACTIVITY 5
2-4 children

- *Creating and drawing symmetrical shapes*
5 × 5 geoboards, elastic bands, geoboard shape paper (PCM 44)
The children create symmetrical shapes on their geoboards, then copy them onto the geoboard paper. They draw a line of symmetry on the shape using a different colour. Point out that it is easier to start with squares and rectangles, then triangles, and progress from there. How many different symmetrical shapes can they make?

ACTIVITY 6
1-2 children

- *Drawing symmetrical shapes and lines of symmetry*
KidPix software (or similar drawing package)
Using KidPix, the children select the symmetry option from the 'wacky brush' tool. They draw a shape and colour it in symmetrically, then use the 'straight line' tool to draw in the lines of symmetry.

S4 3-d shape

ACTIVITY 1
Whole class, in pairs

- *Constructing a cuboid from a net*

Net of a cuboid (PCM 47 photocopied onto card), scissors, glue

The children construct a cuboid from the net. They carefully cut out the net from the card, then score along the fold lines, using a ruler and ball-point pen. Tell them to take great care with the scoring. Finally, they fold along the scored lines and glue the tabs to create a cuboid.

ACTIVITY 2
3 children

- *Drawing a net for a given shape*

Several empty cuboid cardboard boxes, felt-tip pens, scissors

The children take a box, look at each face and discuss what shapes they will see when the box is cut open and spread out flat. Each child then draws the net of the shapes they expect to see. One child carefully cuts open the box along the glue-line seams so that it will spread out flat. What shapes do they see? The children repeat the activity twice more with the other children flattening the boxes.

ACTIVITY 3
2-4 children

- *Constructing a cube from a net*

2 cm-squared paper, sticky tape, felt-tip pens, scissors

Each child draws nets of four cubes on the squared paper: the first where each square face is 2×2 squares, the second is 3×3 squares, the third is 4×4 squares, and the fourth is 5×5 squares. They colour each net in a different colour. They cut out the nets and fold them into cubes, using the sticky tape to make tabs and stick the sides together. They leave each 'lid' open, i.e. they do not stick down the top of the boxes. They then fit one cube inside another so that they have a set of four 'nested' cubes.

ACTIVITY 4
3-4 children

- *Constructing 3-d shapes*
- *Naming and describing the properties of 3-d shapes*

Polydron (squares, rectangles, pentagons, hexagons, triangles), blank cards

The children investigate making different solid shapes with the Polydron. They discuss the names and properties (faces, edges, vertices) of each, and make labels to put next to the completed shapes.

ACTIVITY 5
3 children

- *Naming different 3-d shapes*

A set of 3-d shapes, blank cards

The children place the shapes in a line. They make labels for the names of the shapes, shuffle them and place them face down in a pile. They take turns to reveal a label and place it with a matching shape, checking each other's decisions. When all the shapes have been labelled, they shuffle the cards again and repeat.

ACTIVITY 6
2-4 children

- *Investigating different nets of a cube*

2 cm-squared paper, felt-tip pens, scissors, sticky tape

Each child draws the net of a cube. They then work together to find another arrangement of six squares which will fit together to make a net and which can be folded to make a cube. How many different arrangements of six squares can they find which will make cubes? How many arrangements will not make cubes? When they are satisfied with their nets, they cut them out, using the sticky tape as tabs and make up the cubes.

S5 Direction

ACTIVITY 1
Whole class, in pairs

• *Recognising the 8-point compass directions*
A direction compass
The children choose a starting point in the classroom and locate north. In their pairs, one child names a visible object inside or outside the classroom. Their partner has to say in which direction the object lies. They both check whether the direction is correct. Repeat so that each child has ten turns.

ACTIVITY 2
2-4 children

• *Using a compass to describe the direction of chosen objects*
An 8-point paper compass (PCM 48)
As a class, locate north. Bearing in mind the direction of north, the children write at each direction point the name of an object, either inside or outside the classroom, which lies in that direction.

ACTIVITY 3
2-4 children

• *Using a compass to describe the direction of chosen objects*
An 8-point paper compass (PCM 48)
As a class, locate north. The children take turns to say an object in the room. With the help of the paper compass, the others say between which two directions (or in which exact direction) the object lies, e.g. *The clock lies between south and south-west.*

ACTIVITY 4
2-3 children

• *Using a Roamer to describe a journey, using the 8-point compass directions*
A Roamer (pre-set to turn 45 degrees), obstacle course with north marked
The children devise a series of instructions so that the Roamer can navigate the obstacle course, using 8-point compass directions. They program the Roamer by translating the direction changes into equivalent turns. Can the children find the shortest route along the obstacle course?

ACTIVITY 5
Pairs

• *Constructing a map using the 8-point compass directions*
Squared paper
Using the squared paper, the children draw a Treasure Island map with some landmarks, e.g. treasure, cave, and camp, and mark the eight compass points on the map. They should try to make some of the landmarks north, south, east or west of each other, and some north-east, north-west, south-east or south-west of each other. They then write some of the directions of one landmark from another, e.g. 'cave to treasure: south-west; camp to cave: north'.

S6 Angle

ACTIVITY 1
Whole class, in threes or fours

• *Recognising right-angle turns using the 8-point compass directions*
An 8-point paper compass (PCM 48), direction cards (PCM 49), a pointer, counters
Place the pointer facing north on the paper compass. Shuffle the direction cards and place them face down in a pile. The children take turns to reveal the top card, rotate the pointer clockwise so that it is facing the direction stated on the card and count how many right-angles have been turned, e.g. $1\frac{1}{2}$, starting from north each time. The children write down the number of right-angles turned. The child who turns the most right-angles collects a counter. Repeat several times, starting from a different direction each time. The winner is the child who collects the most counters.

ACTIVITY 2
2-4 children

• *Recognising right-angle turns using the minute hand of a clock*
Analogue clock with movable hands, a dice, counters
Set the clock at twelve o'clock. The children take turns to throw the dice and move the minute hand clockwise in the same number of right-angles as the dice throw. They say the new time and the others check. After each move the clock is passed to the next child. If, at the end of the turn the minute hand points to 12, i.e. o'clock, the child collects a counter. The children continue until the clock shows twelve o'clock again. *Who has collected the most counters?*

ACTIVITY 3
2-4 children

• *Recording angles, in degrees, between the hands on a clock face*
Clock faces (PCM 43)
The children draw hands on the clocks to show different o'clock times. They then write the angle, in degrees, between the hands on each clock.

ACTIVITY 4
2-3 children

• *Recognising right-angles in polygons*
Shape cards (PCM 45)
The children look for right-angles on each of the shapes (inside or interior angles only). They mark each right-angle that they find. *Which shapes have more than one right-angle? Which have none? Which has the most right-angles?*

ACTIVITY 5
2-3 children

• *Converting right-angle and part right-angle turns into degrees*
Direction cards (PCM 49)
The children calculate the angle, in degrees, turned by each direction clockwise from north. They write the size of the angle on each card.

ACTIVITY 1
Whole class, in pairs

- *Plotting points on a coordinate grid*

A coordinate grid (PCM 50), two dice (in different colours), counters (in two colours)

One dice represents the first coordinate (distance along), and the other dice represents the second coordinate (distance up). The children take turns to throw both dice together, then place one of their counters on the matching point on the grid. The winner is the first to have three of their counters in any one line.

ACTIVITY 2
2-4 children

- *Reading and plotting coordinates*

A coordinate grid (PCM 50), counters

One child places five counters at different points on the grid. One of the other children says the coordinates of a point which has a counter, e.g. *Three, two*. If it is correct, they remove the counter and keep it; if not, the turn passes to the next child. The children continue until the counters have all been removed. The children play several rounds, taking turns to place five counters. *Who has collected the most counters?*

ACTIVITY 3
2-4 children

- *Reading the coordinates of points on a coordinate grid*

A coordinate grid (PCM 50), two dice (in different colours), ten interlocking cubes

One dice represents the first coordinate (distance along), the other dice represents the second coordinate (distance up). One child places the ten cubes at random points on the grid. The children take turns to throw both dice together. If the coordinates thrown by the dice match the position of one of the cubes, the child who threw the dice takes the cube. The winner is the first to collect five cubes.

ACTIVITY 4
2-3 children

- *Reading the coordinates of points on a coordinate grid*

A coordinate grid (PCM 50)

The children draw a map on the grid and mark about eight landmarks at random points on the grid. They write a list of the landmarks, and write their corresponding coordinate points beside them.

ACTIVITY 5
2-3 children

- *Drawing and describing polygons on a coordinate grid*
- *Reading points on a coordinate grid*

A coordinate grid (PCM 50)

The children draw a polygon on the coordinate grid. They list the coordinates of the vertices of the polygon at the side of the grid, and then write the name of the polygon, together with any of its properties, at the bottom of the grid. Give the children another grid and ask them to draw a different polygon and repeat the activity.

Frequency tables

ACTIVITY 1

Whole class, in two pairs

- *Constructing and interpreting a frequency table*
- *Recalling multiplication facts up to 6×6*

Squared paper, rulers, felt-tip pens, two dice

1	2	3	4	5	6	8	9	10	12	15	16	18	20	24	25	30	36

Each pair copies this chart:
In pairs, one child throws the two dice, and the other child multiplies the numbers thrown and places a tally mark in the matching box. When each pair have thrown the dice at least 50 times, they add the tally marks to make a frequency table. The two pairs compare their results. *Which answers appeared often in both tables?* The two pairs then draw a new frequency table by combining both sets of results. *Which answer appeared most? Which appeared least?* Can they explain why?

ACTIVITY 2

2-3 children

- *Constructing and interpreting a tally chart*

Tally chart (PCM 51), pack of playing cards

The children write the heading 'suit' in the first column on the chart, and label four rows: 'hearts', 'clubs', 'diamonds' and 'spades'. The children shuffle the cards and turn over 30, one at a time. As each card is revealed, one child draws a tally mark alongside its suit on the tally chart. The children have to find a way of checking that only 30 cards have been turned over. When they have completed writing the tallies, they find the totals for each suit and record them on the chart. They discuss the results. Reshuffle the cards, repeat the activity, and compare the two charts.

ACTIVITY 3

2-4 children

- *Constructing and interpreting a frequency table*

Squared paper, rulers, felt-tip pens, TV listings guides

The children copy this chart:

	Monday	Tuesday	Wednesday	Thursday	Friday	Saturday	Sunday
Films							

Using the TV listings guide, they study the television schedule for one week and count how many films appear on each day (on BBC1, BBC2, ITV, and Channel 4), recording the numbers in their chart. *Which channel showed most films on Monday? Which day of the week had the most films?* Repeat the activity for a different week and compare. Ask the children to break the frequency table into periods of time: morning, afternoon, evening, and night. *Which period of the day showed the most films?*

D2 Pictographs

ACTIVITY 1
Whole class, in two pairs

- *Constructing and interpreting a pictograph (one symbol representing two units)*
- *Constructing a tally chart*

A dice, tally chart (PCM 51)

In pairs, the children throw the dice 30 times. They record on the tally chart how many throws occurred of each number. They represent the results in a pictograph, choosing a symbol to represent two throws. They then combine their results with another pair of children, and draw a new pictograph to show the combined data.

ACTIVITY 2
2-3 children

- *Constructing and interpreting a pictograph (one symbol representing two units)*

Interlocking cubes (in four or five colours), a feely bag

The children construct a pictograph to show the colours of a chosen number of cubes, e.g. 30 or 40. They decide on a symbol to represent two cubes. The children put the cubes in the bag and draw them out one at a time, placing them in rows of the same colour. When they have taken out the required cubes, they count each colour of cubes and draw a pictograph to show the results. They then discuss what the pictograph shows.

ACTIVITY 3
2-4 children

- *Constructing and interpreting a pictograph (one symbol representing four units)*
- *Recognising the difference between two dice scores*
- *Constructing a tally chart*

Two dice, tally chart (PCM 51)

The children discuss all the possible differences between the numbers when two dice are thrown together. They label the rows of the tally chart accordingly, i.e. '0, 1, 2, 3, 4, 5,'. They decide on a number of throws, e. g. 50, take turns to throw the dice and complete the chart and totals. They then draw a pictograph to show the results, using a chosen symbol to represent four throws. Finally, they discuss their pictograph.

ACTIVITY 4
2-4 children

- *Constructing and interpreting a pictograph (one symbol representing three units)*

Class registers (or data showing the number of boys and girls in different classes)

The children collect data based on the number of boys and girls in different classes in school. They construct pictographs to show the results, choosing a symbol to represent three children. They can choose to draw a pictograph to show the number of boys in different classes, the number of girls in different classes, the number of boys and girls in a single class, or the number of children in different classes.

D3 Bar graphs

ACTIVITY 1
Whole class, in pairs

- *Constructing and interpreting a bar graph*

A dice (5, 6, 7, 8, 9, 10), blank bar graph (PCM 52), blank tally chart (PCM 51)
The children take turns to throw the dice, recording each throw with a tally mark on the chart. They stop when one row has a total of 15 throws (three gates). Then they draw a bar graph, marking the vertical divisions in twos. They discuss what the bar graph shows.

ACTIVITY 2
2-3 children

- *Constructing and interpreting a bar graph*

A pack of playing cards, blank bar graph (PCM 52)
The children shuffle the cards, and turn over 20 of them. They separate them into suits, then draw a bar graph to show how many there are of each suit. They label the vertical axis in ones. They replace the cards, reshuffle them and turn over 40, drawing a new bar graph, but labelling the vertical axis in twos.

ACTIVITY 3
2-4 children

- *Constructing and interpreting a bar graph*

Two dice (5, 6, 7, 8, 9, 10), blank bar graph (PCM 52), blank tally chart (PCM 51)
The children investigate the results of throwing two dice together and finding the difference between the numbers thrown. They throw the dice 50 times and record the results in a tally chart. They then draw a bar graph marking the vertical divisions in twos.

ACTIVITY 4
Pairs

- *Using computer software to present data graphically*

Graph-plotting computer software
The children conduct a simple survey, such as the type of pets their classmates have, or what cereals they eat for breakfast, recording their data in a frequency table. They transfer the data to simple graphing software to present their findings pictorially. The children choose an appropriate display, print it and add any missing features (title, labels etc), then give a short report of their findings (either word-processed or hand-written). The report and graph can be combined by cutting and sticking or electronically, according to the children's computer skills.

ACTIVITY 5
2-4 children

- *Constructing and interpreting a bar graph*
- *Collecting and processing data*

Class lists, blank bar graph (PCM 52), blank tally chart (PCM 51)
The children investigate the number of letters in the first names of the children in school. They investigate as many classes as they can, using class lists, recording their results on the tally chart. Finally, they draw a bar graph to illustrate the results, marking the vertical divisions in either twos, fives or tens, depending on how much data they have collected. Extend the activity to cover surnames.

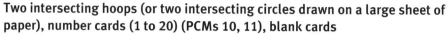

ACTIVITY 1
Whole class, in pairs

• *Sorting numbers using a Venn diagram (two intersecting sets)*
Two intersecting hoops (or two intersecting circles drawn on a large sheet of paper), number cards (1 to 20) (PCMs 10, 11), blank cards
With the blank cards, the children make two labels 'Odd' and 'Multiple of 3' and place them each beside a hoop. They sort the number cards, placing them in the correct area of the hoops, then make a record of the sorted numbers. They can experiment with different labels, e.g. 'Multiple of 4', '2-digit number', 'Even', or 'Divides into 15'.

ACTIVITY 2
2-3 children

• *Sorting cards using a Carroll diagram*
A large 2 × 2 grid drawn on a large sheet of paper, a pack of playing cards, blank cards
Using the blank cards, the children write pairs of labels, e.g. 'red', 'black' and 'picture', 'not a picture'. They place one pair at the top sections of the grid and the other pair at the left side of the grid. They shuffle the cards, and turn them over, one at a time, placing them in their correct position on the grid. They stop when they have placed 20 cards. Repeat the activity using a different pair of labels, e.g. '7 or less', 'more than 7' or 'heart', 'not a heart'.

ACTIVITY 3
2-4 children

• *Sorting shapes using a Venn diagram (two intersecting sets)*
• *Recognising the properties of 2-d shapes*
Two intersecting hoops (or two intersecting circles drawn on a large sheet of paper), shape cards (PCM 45), blank cards
Using the cards, the children make the labels 'regular' and 'less than 5 sides', and place one in each hoop. They shuffle the cards, place them face down, and take turns to pick a shape, placing it in the correct area of the hoops. The other children check that the cards have been placed correctly. Continue until all the shapes have been placed. The children then describe the shapes in each area. Repeat the activity for different labels, e.g. 'quadrilateral' and 'has symmetry'.

ACTIVITY 4
2-4 children

• *Sorting shapes using a Venn diagram (three intersecting sets)*
Three intersecting hoops (or three intersecting circles drawn on a large sheet of paper), number cards (1 to 20) (PCMs 10, 11), blank cards
Using the cards, the children make three labels 'Odd', 'Multiple of 3' and 'More than 9', and place them each beside a hoop. They sort the number cards, placing them in their correct area, then make a record of the sorted numbers. Let them experiment with different labels, e.g. 'Multiple of 4', 'Even', 'Divides into 24', 'Between 5 and 15'.

1	0		
2	0	0	b
3	0	0	8
4	0	0	7
5	0	0	9

Abacus Ginn and Company 2000. Copying permitted for purchasing school only. This material is not copyright free.

1	0	0	5
2	0	0	4
3	0	0	3
4	0	0	2
5	0	0	1

Abacus Ginn and Company 2000. Copying permitted for purchasing school only. This material is not copyright free.

6	0	0	b
7	0	0	8
8	0	0	7
q	0	0	9

Abacus Ginn and Company 2000. Copying permitted for purchasing school only. This material is not copyright free.

1 0 0 0

2 0 0 0

3 0 0 0

4 0 0 0

5 0 0 0

Abacus Ginn and Company 2000. Copying permitted for purchasing school only. This material is not copyright free.

6 0 0 0

7 0 0 0

8 0 0 0

9 0 0 0

Abacus Ginn and Company 2000. Copying permitted for purchasing school only. This material is not copyright free.

			· 0	1
b 0	·	· 0	2
8 0	·	· 0	3
7 0	·	· 0	4
9 0	·	· 0	5

Abacus Ginn and Company 2000. Copying permitted for purchasing school only. This material is not copyright free.

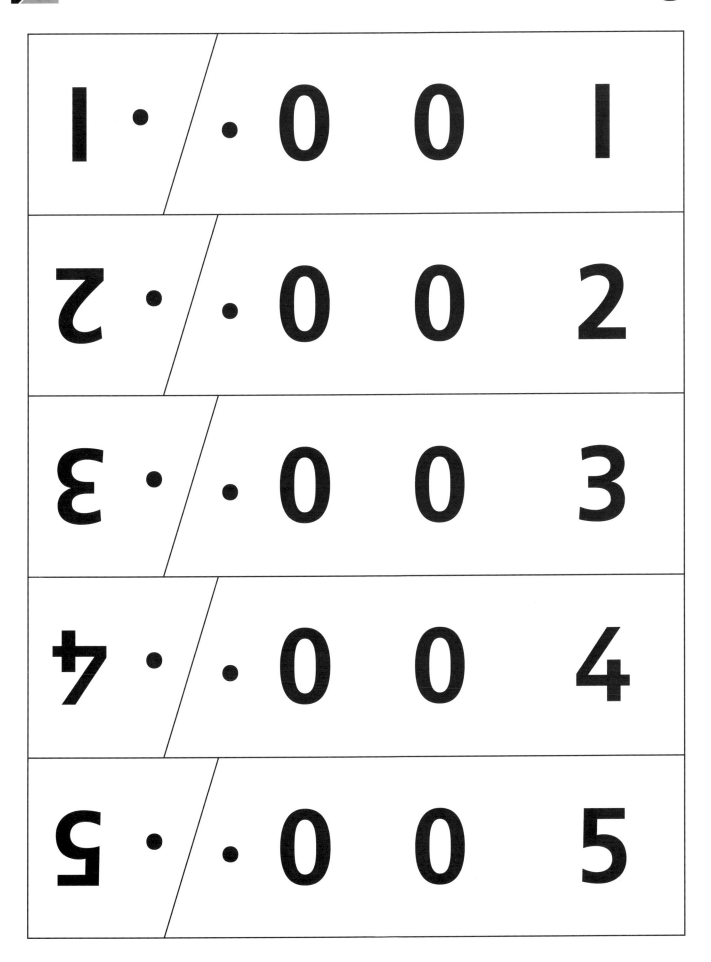

Abacus Ginn and Company 2000. Copying permitted for purchasing school only. This material is not copyright free.

9 · / · 0   0   6

7 · / · 0   0   7

8 · / · 0   0   8

b · / · 0   0   q

Abacus Ginn and Company 2000. Copying permitted for purchasing school only. This material is not copyright free.

0 1 2 3 4 5 6 7 8 9 10 11 12 13 14 15 16 17 18 19 20

21 22 23 24 25 26 27 28 29 30 31 32 33 34 35 36 37 38 39 40

Attach here

41 42 43 44 45 46 47 48 49 50 51 52 53 54 55 56 57 58 59 60

Attach here

61 62 63 64 65 66 67 68 69 70 71 72 73 74 75 76 77 78 79 80

Attach here

81 82 83 84 85 86 87 88 89 90 91 92 93 94 95 96 97 98 99 100

Attach here

Abacus Ginn and Company 2000. Copying permitted for purchasing school only. This material is not copyright free.

0	1	2
3	4	5
6	7	8
9	10	

Abacus Ginn and Company 2000. Copying permitted for purchasing school only. This material is not copyright free.

11	12	13
14	15	16
17	18	19
20		

Abacus Ginn and Company 2000. Copying permitted for purchasing school only. This material is not copyright free.

21	**22**	**23**	**24**
25	**26**	**27**	**28**
29	**30**	**31**	**32**
33	**34**	**35**	**36**

Abacus Ginn and Company 2000. Copying permitted for purchasing school only. This material is not copyright free.

37	38	39	40
41	42	43	44
45	46	47	48
49	50	51	52

Abacus Ginn and Company 2000. Copying permitted for purchasing school only. This material is not copyright free.

53	54	55	56
57	58	59	60
61	62	63	64
65	66	67	68

Abacus Ginn and Company 2000. Copying permitted for purchasing school only. This material is not copyright free.

69	**70**	**71**	**72**
73	**74**	**75**	**76**
77	**78**	**79**	**80**
81	**82**	**83**	**84**

Abacus Ginn and Company 2000. Copying permitted for purchasing school only. This material is not copyright free.

85	86	87	88
89	90	91	92
93	94	95	96
97	98	99	100

Abacus Ginn and Company 2000. Copying permitted for purchasing school only. This material is not copyright free.

110	120	130
140	150	160
170	180	190
	200	

Abacus Ginn and Company 2000. Copying permitted for purchasing school only. This material is not copyright free.

210	220	230
240	250	260
270	280	290
	300	

Abacus Ginn and Company 2000. Copying permitted for purchasing school only. This material is not copyright free.

1	2	3	4	5	6	7	8	9	10
11	12	13	14	15	16	17	18	19	20
21	22	23	24	25	26	27	28	29	30
31	32	33	34	35	36	37	38	39	40
41	42	43	44	45	46	47	48	49	50
51	52	53	54	55	56	57	58	59	60
61	62	63	64	65	66	67	68	69	70
71	72	73	74	75	76	77	78	79	80
81	82	83	84	85	86	87	88	89	90
91	92	93	94	95	96	97	98	99	100

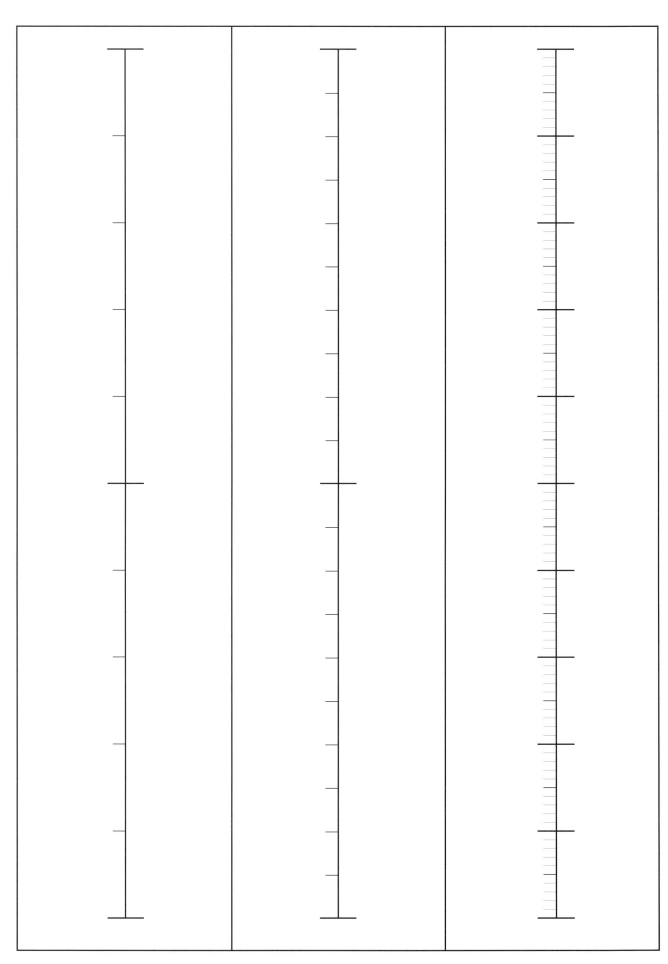

Abacus Ginn and Company 2000. Copying permitted for purchasing school only. This material is not copyright free.

4

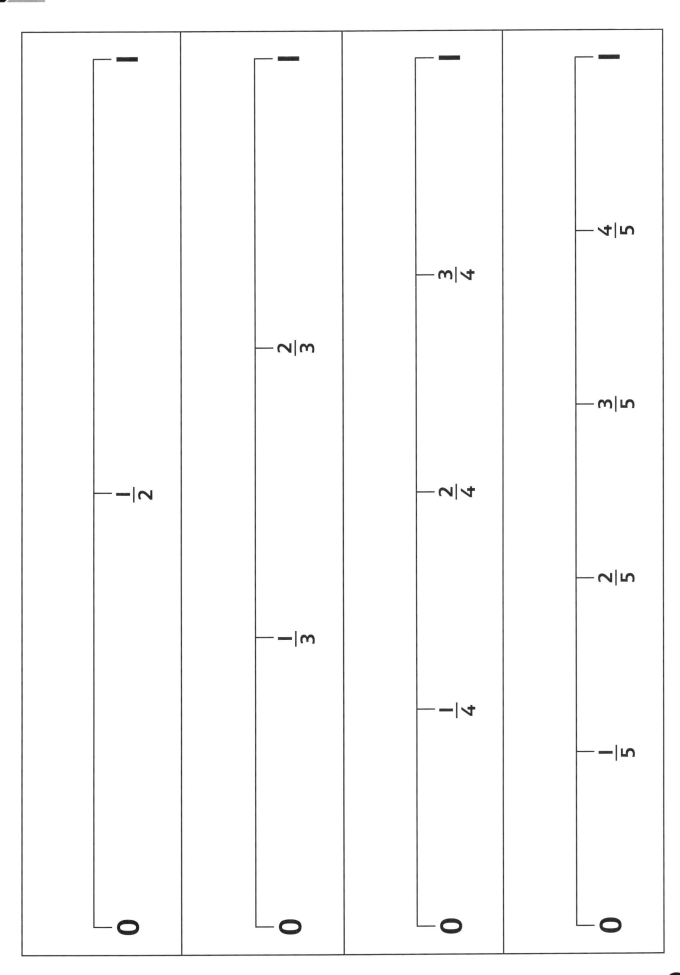

Abacus Ginn and Company 2000. Copying permitted for purchasing school only. This material is not copyright free.

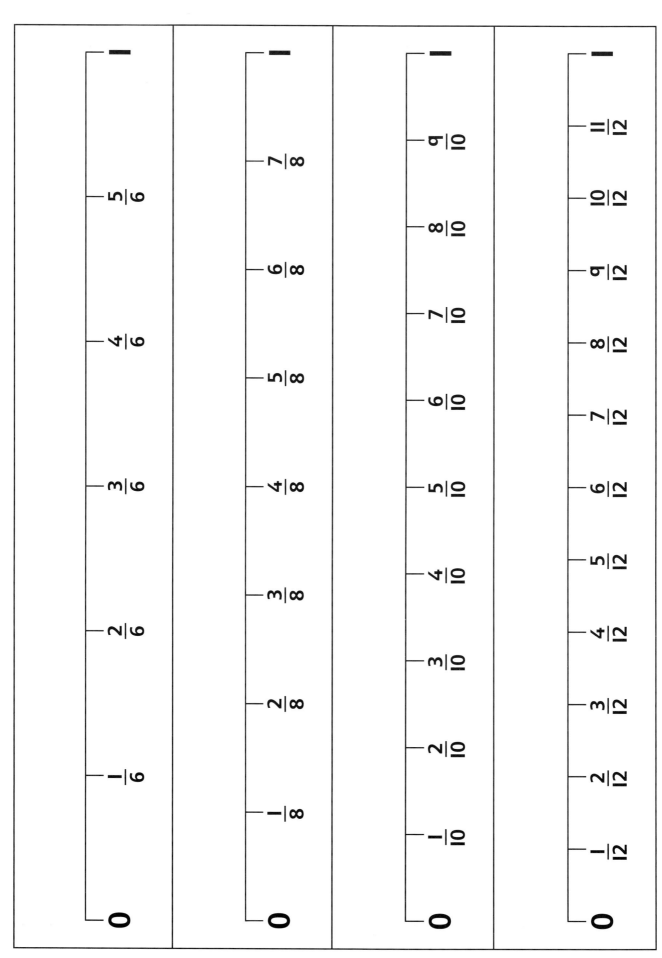

Abacus Ginn and Company 2000. Copying permitted for purchasing school only. This material is not copyright free.

U (Units)	T (Tens)	H (Hundreds)	T (Thousands)

Abacus Ginn and Company 2000. Copying permitted for purchasing school only. This material is not copyright free.

×10	10	20	30	40	50	60	70	80	90	100
×9	9	18	27	36	45	54	63	72	81	90
×8	8	16	24	32	40	48	56	64	72	80
×7	7	14	21	28	35	42	49	56	63	70
×6	6	12	18	24	30	36	42	48	54	60
×5	5	10	15	20	25	30	35	40	45	50
×4	4	8	12	16	20	24	28	32	36	40
×3	3	6	9	12	15	18	21	24	27	30
×2	2	4	6	8	10	12	14	16	18	20

Abacus Ginn and Company 2000. Copying permitted for purchasing school only. This material is not copyright free.

1	2			5	6	7	8	9	10
2	4	6	8	10	12	14	16	18	20
3	6	9	12	15	18	21	24	27	30
4	8	12	16	20	24	28	32	36	40
5	10	15	20	25	30	35	40	45	50
6	12	18	24	30	36	42	48	54	60
7	14	21	28	35	42	49	56	63	70
8	16	24	32	40	48	56	64	72	80
9	18	27	36	45	54	63	72	81	90
10	20	30	40	50	60	70	80	90	100

Abacus Ginn and Company 2000. Copying permitted for purchasing school only. This material is not copyright free.

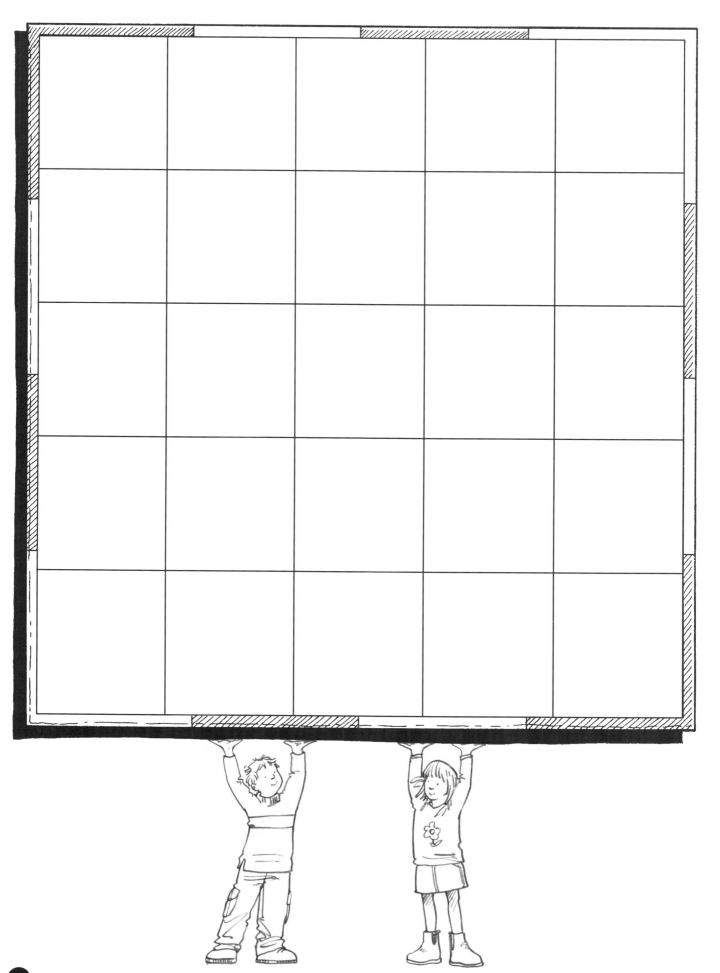

Abacus Ginn and Company 2000. Copying permitted for purchasing school only. This material is not copyright free.

10	20	30	40	50	60	70	80	90	100
110	120	130	140	150	160	170	180	190	200
210	220	230	240	250	260	270	280	290	300
310	320	330	340	350	360	370	380	390	400
410	420	430	440	450	460	470	480	490	500
510	520	530	540	550	560	570	580	590	600
610	620	630	640	650	660	670	680	690	700
710	720	730	740	750	760	770	780	790	800
810	820	830	840	850	860	870	880	890	900
910	920	930	940	950	960	970	980	990	1000

Abacus Ginn and Company 2000. Copying permitted for purchasing school only. This material is not copyright free.

Abacus Ginn and Company 2000. Copying permitted for purchasing school only. This material is not copyright free.

4

Abacus Ginn and Company 2000. Copying permitted for purchasing school only. This material is not copyright free.

=

Abacus Ginn and Company 2000. Copying permitted for purchasing school only. This material is not copyright free.

$\frac{1}{2}$	$\frac{1}{2}$	$\frac{1}{4}$
$\frac{1}{4}$	$\frac{2}{3}$	$\frac{2}{3}$
$\frac{3}{4}$	$\frac{3}{4}$	$\frac{3}{5}$
$\frac{3}{5}$	$\frac{1}{10}$	$\frac{1}{10}$

Abacus Ginn and Company 2000. Copying permitted for purchasing school only. This material is not copyright free.

$\dfrac{2}{6}$	$\dfrac{2}{8}$	$\dfrac{5}{10}$
$\dfrac{6}{12}$	$\dfrac{3}{6}$	$\dfrac{4}{8}$
$\dfrac{3}{12}$	$\dfrac{8}{12}$	$\dfrac{4}{6}$
$\dfrac{6}{8}$	$\dfrac{4}{12}$	$\dfrac{9}{12}$

Abacus Ginn and Company 2000. Copying permitted for purchasing school only. This material is not copyright free.

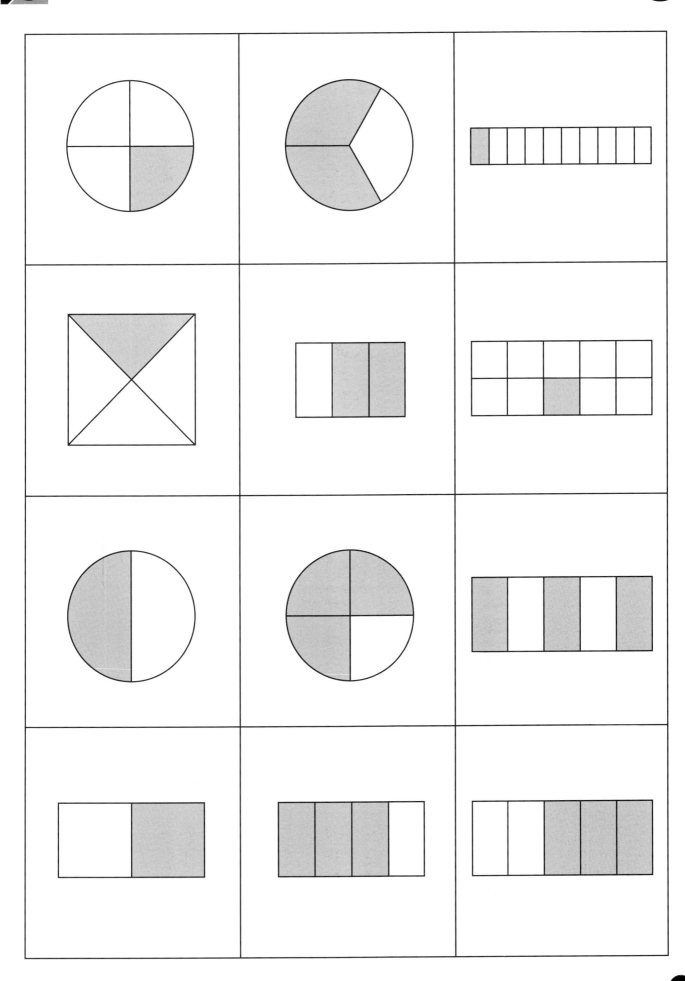

Abacus Ginn and Company 2000. Copying permitted for purchasing school only. This material is not copyright free.

4

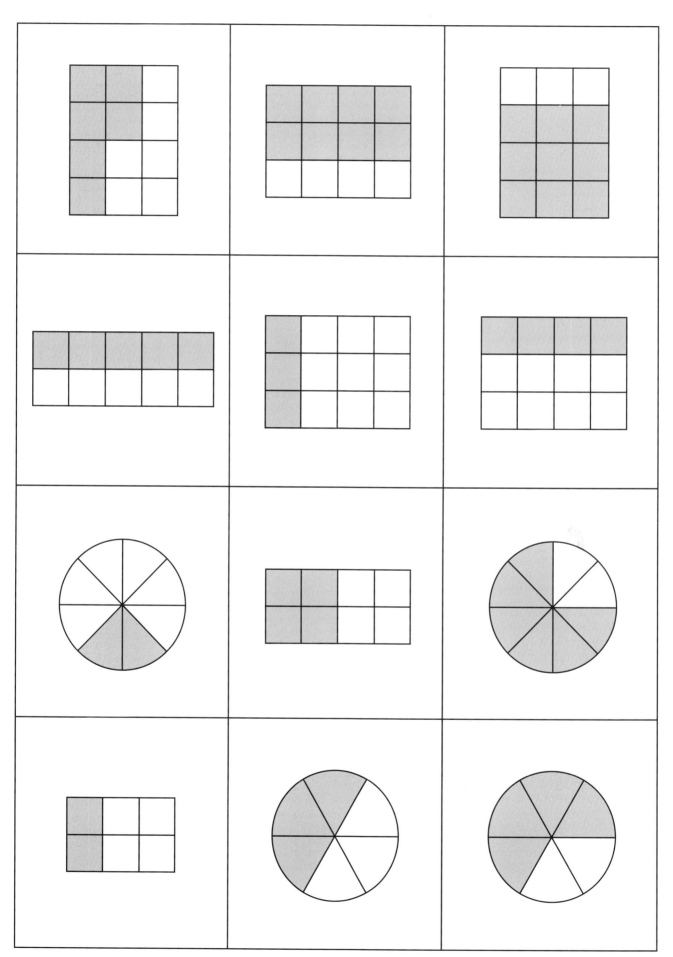

Abacus Ginn and Company 2000. Copying permitted for purchasing school only. This material is not copyright free.

4×3	8×3	2×4	6×4
3×3	7×3	1×4	5×4
2×3	6×3	10×3	4×4
1×3	5×3	9×3	3×4

Abacus Ginn and Company 2000. Copying permitted for purchasing school only. This material is not copyright free.

10×4	4×6	8×6	2×7
9×4	3×6	7×6	1×7
8×4	2×6	6×6	10×6
7×4	1×6	5×6	9×6

Abacus Ginn and Company 2000. Copying permitted for purchasing school only. This material is not copyright free.

6×7	10×7	4×8	8×8
5×7	9×7	3×8	7×8
4×7	8×7	2×8	6×8
3×7	7×7	1×8	5×8

Abacus Ginn and Company 2000. Copying permitted for purchasing school only. This material is not copyright free.

2×9	1×9	10×8	9×8
6×9	5×9	4×9	3×9
10×9	9×9	8×9	7×9

Abacus Ginn and Company 2000. Copying permitted for purchasing school only. This material is not copyright free.

$12 \div 3$	$24 \div 3$	$8 \div 4$	$24 \div 4$
$9 \div 3$	$21 \div 3$	$4 \div 4$	$20 \div 4$
$6 \div 3$	$18 \div 3$	$30 \div 3$	$16 \div 4$
$3 \div 3$	$15 \div 3$	$27 \div 3$	$12 \div 4$

Abacus Ginn and Company 2000. Copying permitted for purchasing school only. This material is not copyright free.

40 ÷ 4	24 ÷ 6	48 ÷ 6	14 ÷ 7
36 ÷ 4	18 ÷ 6	42 ÷ 6	7 ÷ 7
32 ÷ 4	12 ÷ 6	36 ÷ 6	60 ÷ 6
28 ÷ 4	6 ÷ 6	30 ÷ 6	54 ÷ 6

Abacus Ginn and Company 2000. Copying permitted for purchasing school only. This material is not copyright free.

42 ÷ 7	70 ÷ 7	32 ÷ 8	64 ÷ 8
35 ÷ 7	63 ÷ 7	24 ÷ 8	56 ÷ 8
28 ÷ 7	56 ÷ 7	16 ÷ 8	48 ÷ 8
21 ÷ 7	49 ÷ 7	8 ÷ 8	40 ÷ 8

Abacus Ginn and Company 2000. Copying permitted for purchasing school only. This material is not copyright free.

18 ÷ 9	54 ÷ 9	90 ÷ 9	
9 ÷ 9	45 ÷ 9	81 ÷ 9	
80 ÷ 8	36 ÷ 9	72 ÷ 9	
72 ÷ 8	27 ÷ 9	63 ÷ 9	

Abacus Ginn and Company 2000. Copying permitted for purchasing school only. This material is not copyright free.

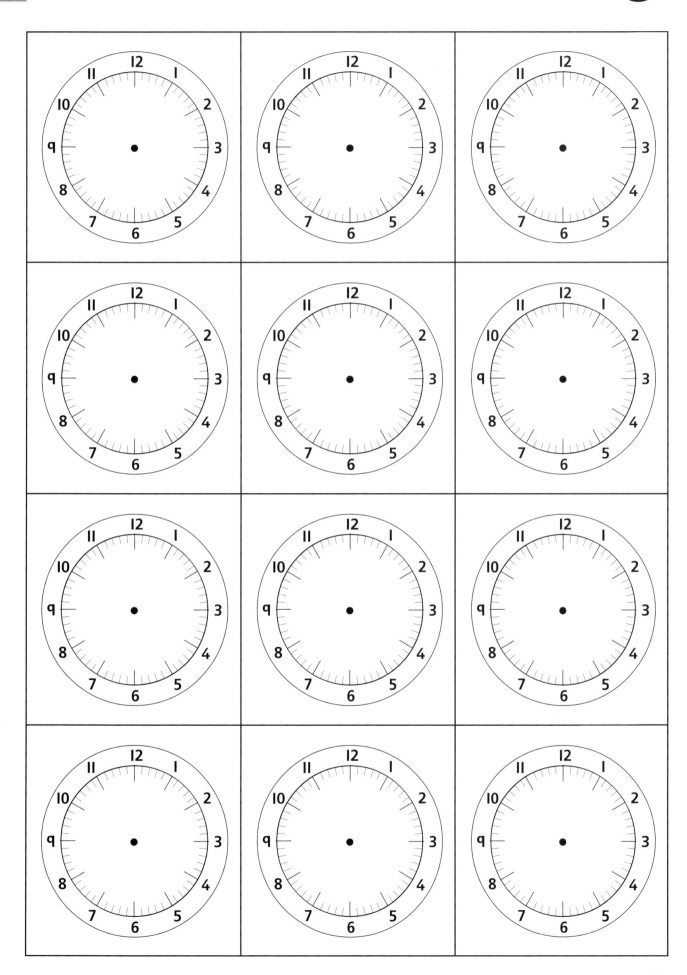

4

Abacus Ginn and Company 2000. Copying permitted for purchasing school only. This material is not copyright free.

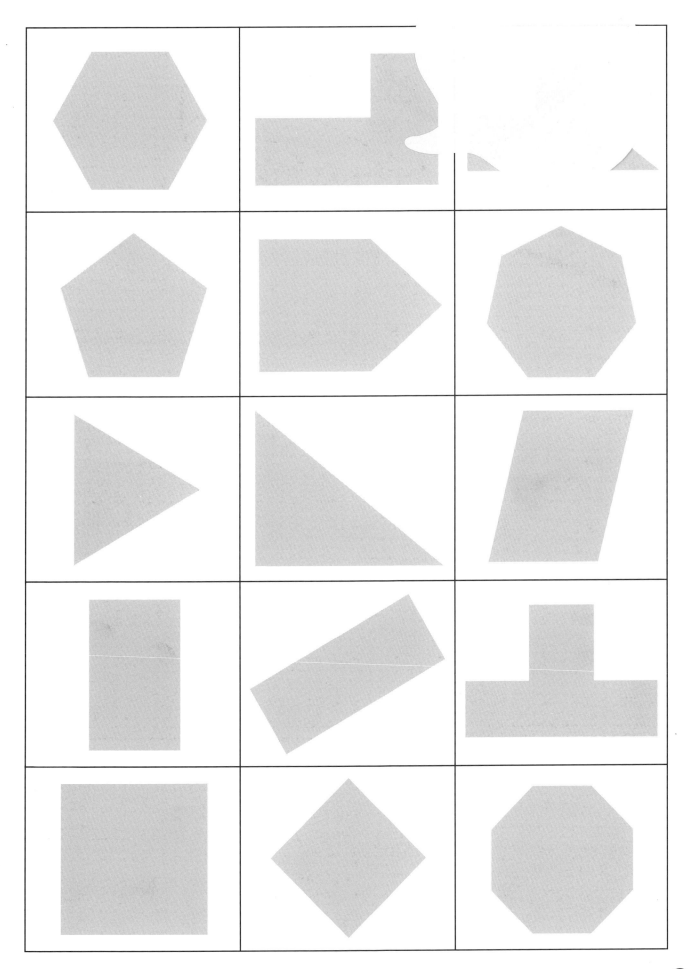

Abacus Ginn and Company 2000. Copying permitted for purchasing school only. This material is not copyright free.

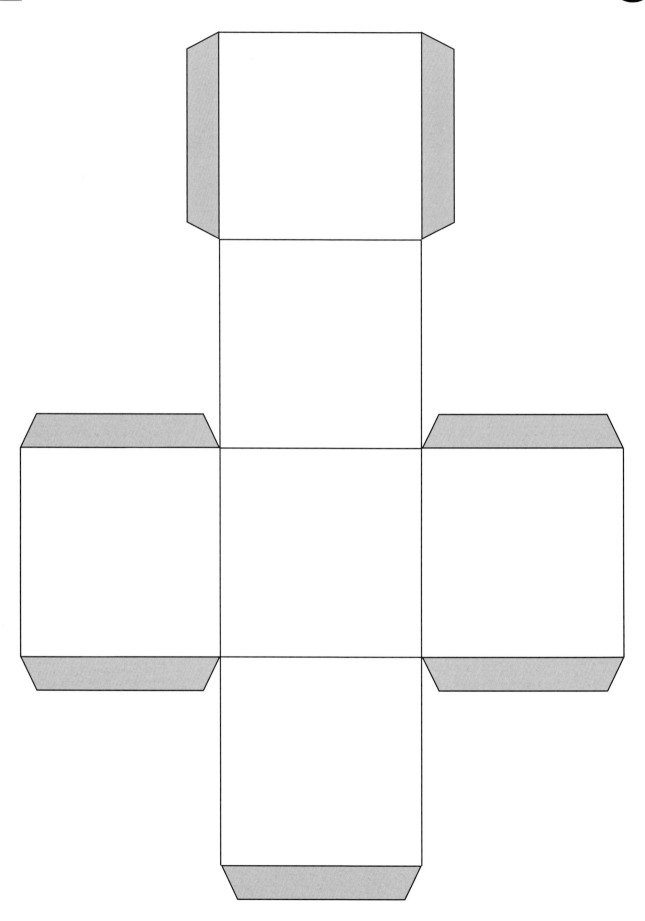

Abacus Ginn and Company 2000. Copying permitted for purchasing school only. This material is not copyright free.

4

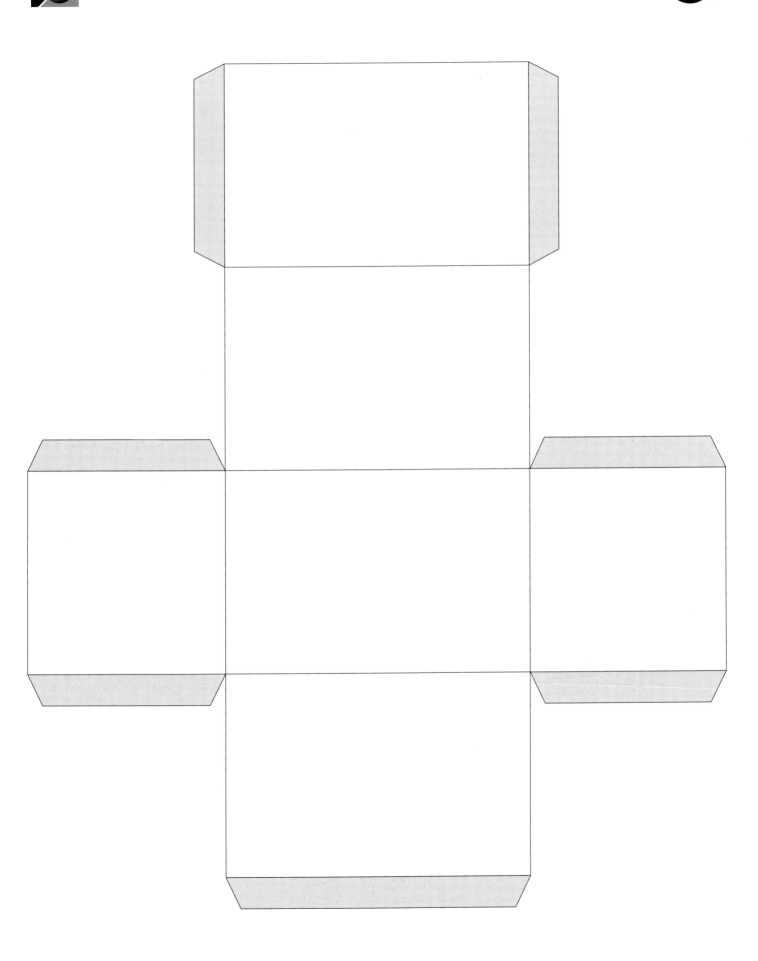

Abacus Ginn and Company 2000. Copying permitted for purchasing school only. This material is not copyright free.

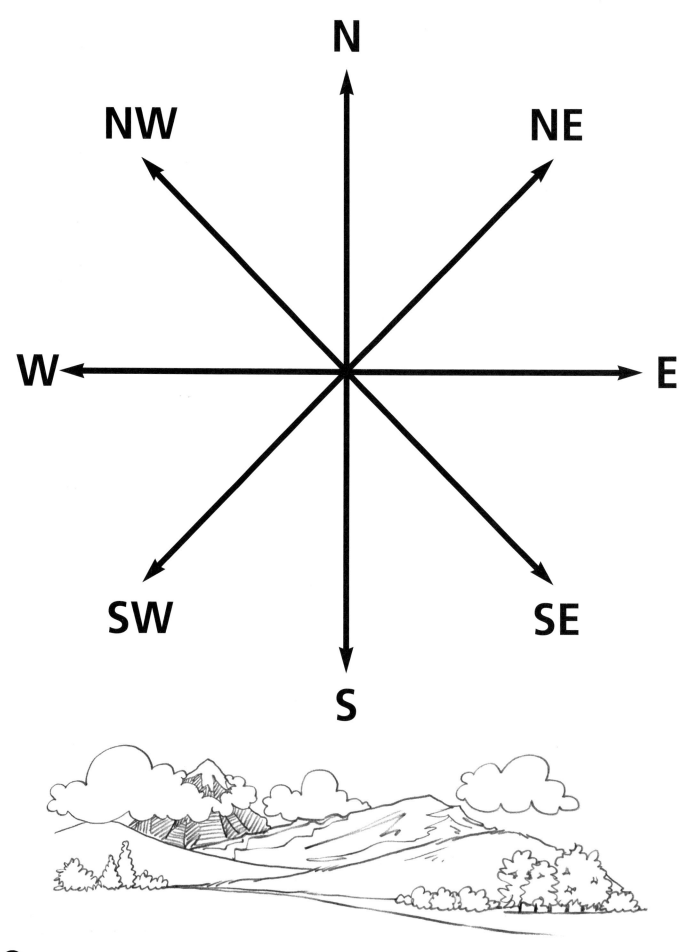

Abacus Ginn and Company 2000. Copying permitted for purchasing school only. This material is not copyright free.

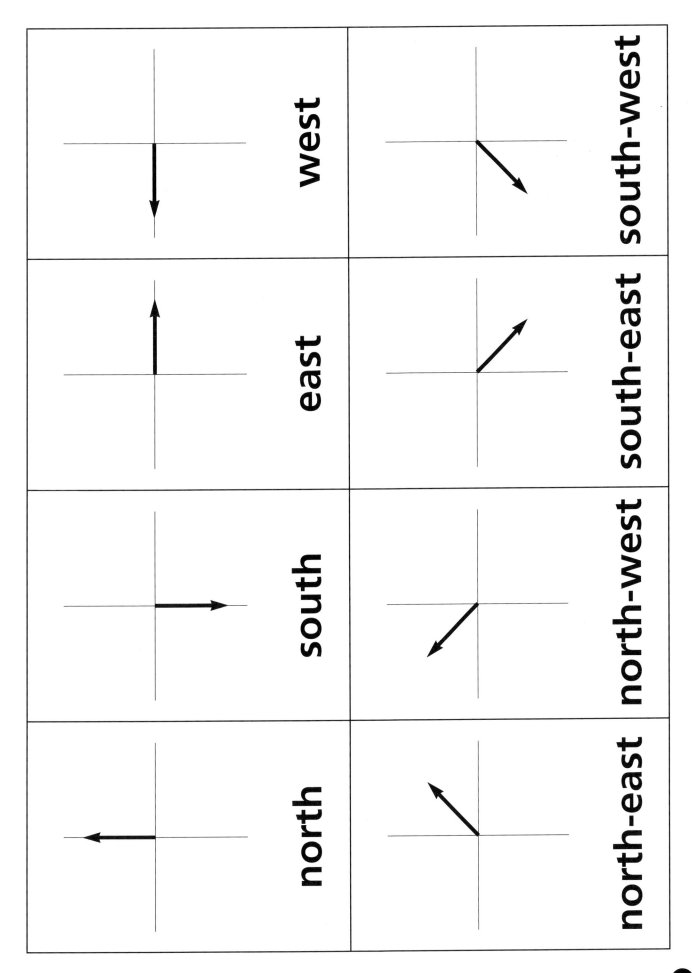

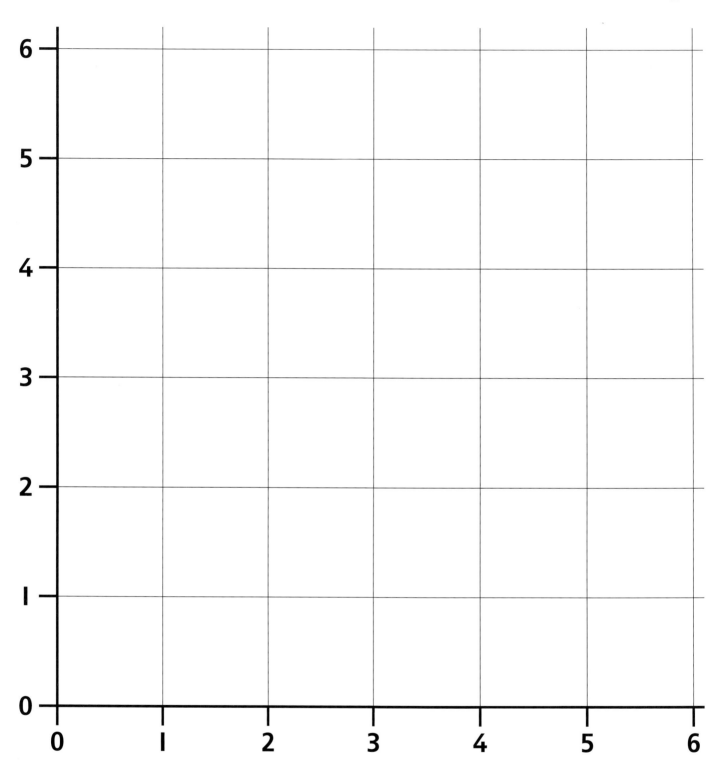

Abacus Ginn and Company 2000. Copying permitted for purchasing school only. This material is not copyright free.

Title:

Total	Tallies	

Abacus Ginn and Company 2000. Copying permitted for purchasing school only. This material is not copyright free.

Title: _____

Abacus Ginn and Company 2000. Copying permitted for purchasing school only. This material is not copyright free.

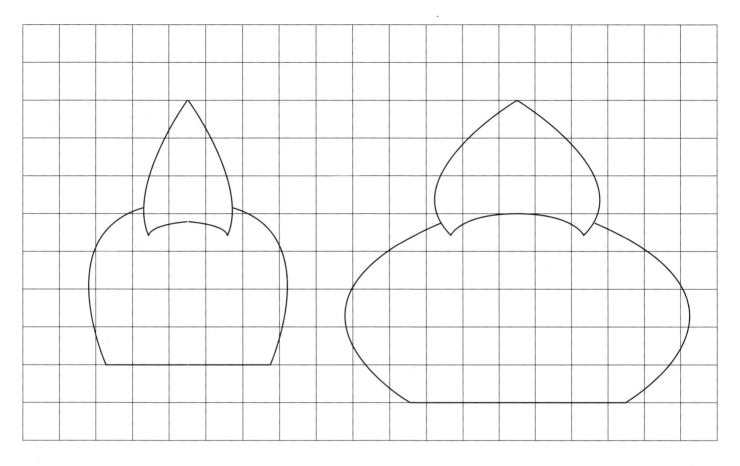

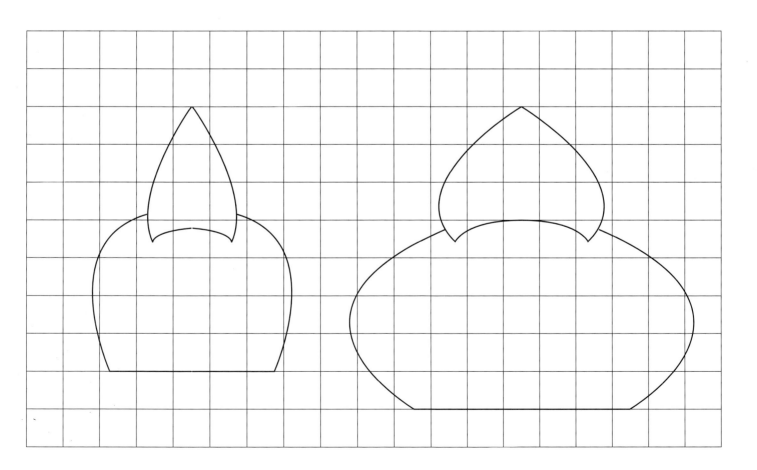

Abacus Ginn and Company 2000. Copying permitted for purchasing school only. This material is not copyright free.

Destination	Times										
Gotham City Centre	9:30	10:30	11:30	3:30	4:40	5:00					
Empire State Building	9:45	10:45	11:45	3:45	4:55	5:15					
Central Park	9:52	10:52	11:52	3:52	5:02	5:22					
Brooklyn Bridge	10:03	11:03	12:03	4:03	5:13	5:33					
The Bronx	10:14	11:14	12:14	4:14	5:24	5:44					
Harlem	10:25	11:25	12:25	4:25	5:35	5:55					
Greenwich Village	10:42	11:42	12:42	4:42	5:52	6:12					
Fifth Avenue	11:01	12:01	1:01	5:01	6:11	6:31					
Broadway	11:30	12:30	1:30	5:30	6:40	7:00					

Abacus Ginn and Company 2000. Copying permitted for purchasing school only. This material is not copyright free.